DK

Dinosaur A to Z

Written by Dustin Growick
Consultant: Darren Naish

DK | Penguin Random House

Senior editor Marie Greenwood
Designer Lucy Sims
Jacket co-ordinator Francesca Young
Jacket designer Amy Keast
Managing editor Laura Gilbert
Managing art editor Diane Peyton Jones
Pre-production producer Dragana Puvacic
Producer Isabell Schart
Art director Martin Wilson
Publisher Sarah Larter
Publishing director Sophie Mitchell

Designed, edited and project-managed
for DK by Dynamo Ltd.

First published in Great Britain in 2017 by
Dorling Kindersley Limited
80 Strand, London, WC2R 0RL

Copyright © 2017 Dorling Kindersley Limited.
A Penguin Random House Company
10 9 8 7 6 5 4 3 2 1
001-298821-Oct/2017

A CIP catalogue record for this book
is available from the British Library

ISBN: 978-0-2412-8387-5

Printed and bound in China

A WORLD OF IDEAS:
SEE ALL THERE IS TO KNOW

www.dk.com

Contents

How this book works

Follow a parade of dinosaurs from Abelisaurus to Zuniceratops! Each page is packed with information about the biggest, smallest, and most interesting dinosaurs that walked the Earth.

Extra dinosaur facts are dotted throughout.

Pronunciation

No need to get your tongue twisted trying to say dinosaur names. Look for the simple pronunciation guide for each dinosaur in the parade.

Where did they get their names?

Find out what each dinosaur name means. Often, the meaning gives a clue to a feature of the dinosaur or where it was found.

Details

Get the low-down on each dinosaur – find out which dinosaurs were related, what they ate, and what made each one special. Key features are highlighted in bold.

Edmontosaurus

ed-MON-toe-SAW-russ

Edmonton lizard

Edmontosaurus had a **very long skull**, which could measure more than a metre (3 ft 3 in) in length. A big skull meant it could have a big mouth with **hundreds of teeth** arranged in long rows. These teeth were continuously being worn down and replaced throughout its life.

Edmontosaurus moved its **lower jaw backwards and forwards** when chewing food.

Edmontosaurus lived in western North America.

Edmontosaurus was one of the largest of its group, called the hadrosaurs.

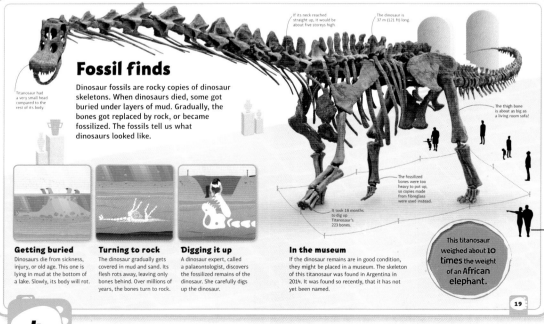

Fossil finds

Dinosaur fossils are rocky copies of dinosaur skeletons. When dinosaurs died, some got buried under layers of mud. Gradually, the bones got replaced by rock, or became fossilized. The fossils tell us what dinosaurs looked like.

Titanosaur had a very small head compared to the rest of its body.

If its neck reached straight up, it would be about five storeys high.

The dinosaur is 37 m (121 ft) long.

The thigh bone is about as big as a living room sofa!

The fossilized bones were too heavy to put up, so copies made from fibreglass were used instead.

It took 18 months to dig up Titanosaur's 223 bones.

This titanosaur weighed about **10 times** the weight of an **African elephant.**

Getting buried
Dinosaurs die from sickness, injury, or old age. This one is lying in mud at the bottom of a lake. Slowly, its body will rot.

Turning to rock
The dinosaur gradually gets covered in mud and sand. Its flesh rots away, leaving only bones behind. Over millions of years, the bones turn to rock.

Digging it up
A dinosaur expert, called a palaeontologist, discovers the fossilized remains of the dinosaur. She carefully digs up the dinosaur.

In the museum
If the dinosaur remains are in good condition, they might be placed in a museum. The skeleton of this titanosaur was found in Argentina in 2014. It was found so recently, that it has not yet been named.

19

You'll find feature pages on dinosaurs and their prehistoric world scattered throughout.

Flying reptiles have joined the parade too!

Scale

All the dinosaurs walking across the page are in proportion with each other. This means you might only see the legs of some of the tallest creatures!

Look out for plants and trees from the time of the dinosaurs.

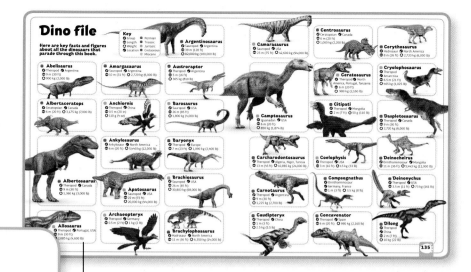

Check out the fact file pages at the back for dinosaur facts and figures.

See how you measure up against your favourite dinosaurs!

If an animal has its eyes set facing out to the sides, it's probably a plant-eater.

Eryops
ear-ee-ops
Drawn-out face

Eryops might have looked like a slow, fat amphibian, but this animal was **to be feared**. It had a massive skull, **long, strong jaws**, and teeth on the roof of its mouth. Any prey it caught would have found it nearly **impossible to escape**.

NOT A DINOSAUR

Eryops' limbs stuck out from the side of its body. This is a clear sign it was not a dinosaur.

At a glance

Each dinosaur is colour coded, so you know which period they came from. Keep your eyes peeled though, some non-dinosaurs from prehistoric times have snuck into the parade. Look out for the blue and green lines - they don't appear very often!

Permian

Triassic

Jurassic

Cretaceous

Miocene

Not a dinosaur?

Some of the animals featured in this book aren't technically dinosaurs – but they are still important to learn about. Look out for this stamp!

Watch out for modern-day animals to see how they compare size-wise.

Some dinosaurs had very small heads compared to the rest of their body.

Birds belong to the **dinosaur** family, too!

What is a dinosaur?

The name dinosaur means "terrible lizard". However, dinosaurs weren't really lizards at all! This diverse group of animals range in size from not much bigger than a sparrow to three times the height of a giraffe!

Many plant-eating dinosaurs had long necks, which helped them feed from the tallest treetops.

Scales

It was discovered a long time ago that dinosaurs had scales. This was learnt from lots of trace fossils, which have preserved the texture and look of the skin of many different species. Other dinosaurs have feathers, and some have both.

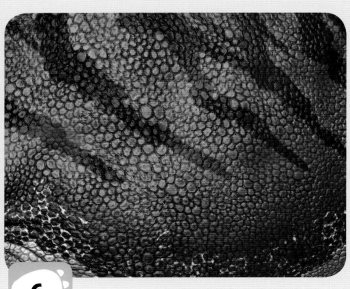

Large dinosaurs needed thick, strong legs to support their weight.

Some dinosaurs, like Diplodocus, walked on four legs. Others walked on two, and used their other two "legs" as arms.

Eggs

As far as we know, all dinosaurs laid eggs. Most clutches, or group of eggs, were small. Some dinosaurs even sat on top of nests to keep their eggs warm, much like birds do today.

This fossilized egg belongs to Aepyornis, or "elephant bird", the biggest bird that ever lived.

Giganotosaurus' tail

Euoplocephalus' tail

Deinonychus' tail

Tails

All dinosaurs had tails, but they were used in very different ways. Some species used them for protection, while others used them as a counter-balance to help when running fast.

Is it a dinosaur?

Not all prehistoric creatures were dinosaurs. Use this flow chart to work out if an animal is, or is not, a dinosaur.

There is one exception to this chart. A group of reptiles called Pseudosuchia also has legs under the body, just like dinosaurs do!

Dinosaurs used their long tails for balance.

Are its legs directly under its body?

Yes!

Does it have scales or feathers?

Yes!

It's a dinosaur!

No...

It's not a dinosaur!

No...

Dinosaur ages

Dinosaurs first appeared on Earth during the Mesozoic Era, which lasted from about 250 million years ago until 66 million years ago. In the Mesozoic Era, the Earth was warmer than it is today, and all the continents were joined in one large landmass called Pangaea.

Heterodontosaurus

Permian

The first reptiles and early forms of mammals appeared in the Permian Era, about 300 million years ago. There were no dinosaurs at this time.

Triassic period: 250–200 million years ago

Large conifers first appeared on Earth during the Triassic period. They grew throughout the Jurassic and Cretaceous periods, too!

Triassic period

Dinosaurs first appeared in this period, which spanned the first 50 million years of the Mesozoic Era.

Jurassic period

During this period, many new types of dinosaur developed, and began to spread out all over the Earth.

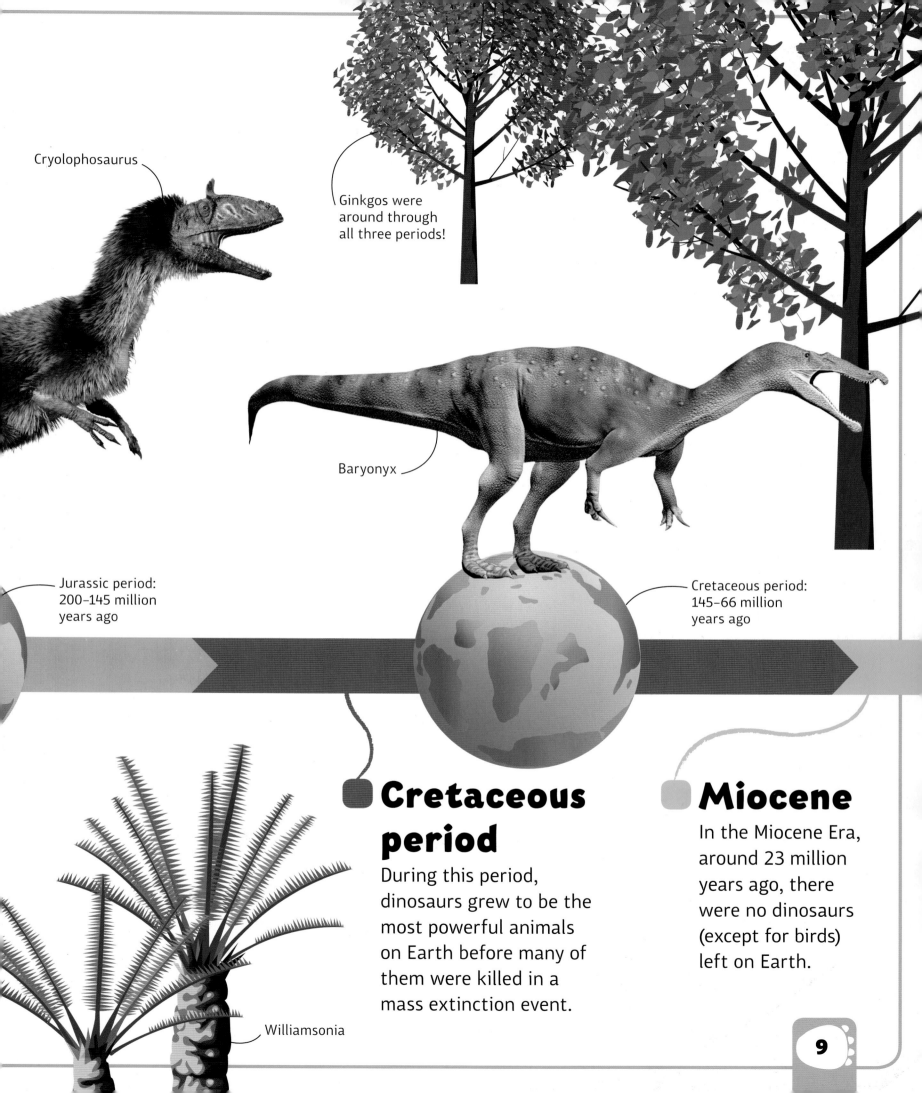

Cryolophosaurus

Ginkgos were around through all three periods!

Baryonyx

Jurassic period: 200–145 million years ago

Cretaceous period: 145–66 million years ago

Cretaceous period

During this period, dinosaurs grew to be the most powerful animals on Earth before many of them were killed in a mass extinction event.

Miocene

In the Miocene Era, around 23 million years ago, there were no dinosaurs (except for birds) left on Earth.

Williamsonia

9

Dinosaur groups

There were many different kinds of dinosaurs alive during the Mesozoic Era. To help us understand them better, scientists have put dinosaurs into groups according to their features and habits. Here are four of the most well-known groups.

There are many types of dinosaur but most fall into two main categories: **Saurischians** or "lizard-hipped" and **Ornithiscians** or "bird-hipped".

Razor sharp teeth pointed inwards to make sure prey went down the predator's throat.

Theropods

Theropods had powerful leg muscles built for chasing and holding down prey.

Theropods varied in size, but they were all bipeds, walking on two legs. Most were meat-eaters. This group has some of the most famous predators of all time, including Spinosaurus, Velociraptor, and Tyrannosaurus rex.

Special features:

- Sharp claws
- Sharp teeth
- Bipeds

Sauropods

Sauropod heads (and brains) were often very small compared to their bodies.

Sauropods walked on four legs. This plant-eating group included some of the largest animals ever to walk the Earth. Some weighed more than 80 tonnes (88 tons), or 10 elephants!

Special features:
- Long necks
- Long tails
- Massive bodies

Ceratopsians

Ceratopsians were strange-looking dinosaurs, with large heads, crests, spikes, horns, and frills. These plant-eaters often moved in herds. Triceratops is the most famous ceratopsian.

Special features:
- Big heads
- Horns
- Crests and frills

Ceratopsians weren't built to run fast, but they may have travelled long distances.

Ornithopods

This group includes hadrosaurs and their smaller, two-legged relatives Hypsilophodon. Many ornithopods could walk on four or two legs as they searched for plants to eat.

Fossilized skin impressions give us great clues about what Iguanodon's skin looked like.

Special features:
- Lots of teeth
- Beaks
- Fast runners

Abelisaurus

ah-BELL-li-SAW-russ

Abel's lizard

This medium-sized theropod had **short front teeth** and **small bony ridges** on its skull just above its eyes. That's just about all that is known about Abelisaurus. When its remains were uncovered in **Patagonia**, Argentina, all that was found was a skull.

Dinosaurs first appeared on Earth around 250 **million years ago.**

Abelisaurus was a meat-eater that lived about 80 million years ago.

Prehistoric ferns look much like today's ferns.

Abelisaurus, like all theropods, probably walked upright on two legs.

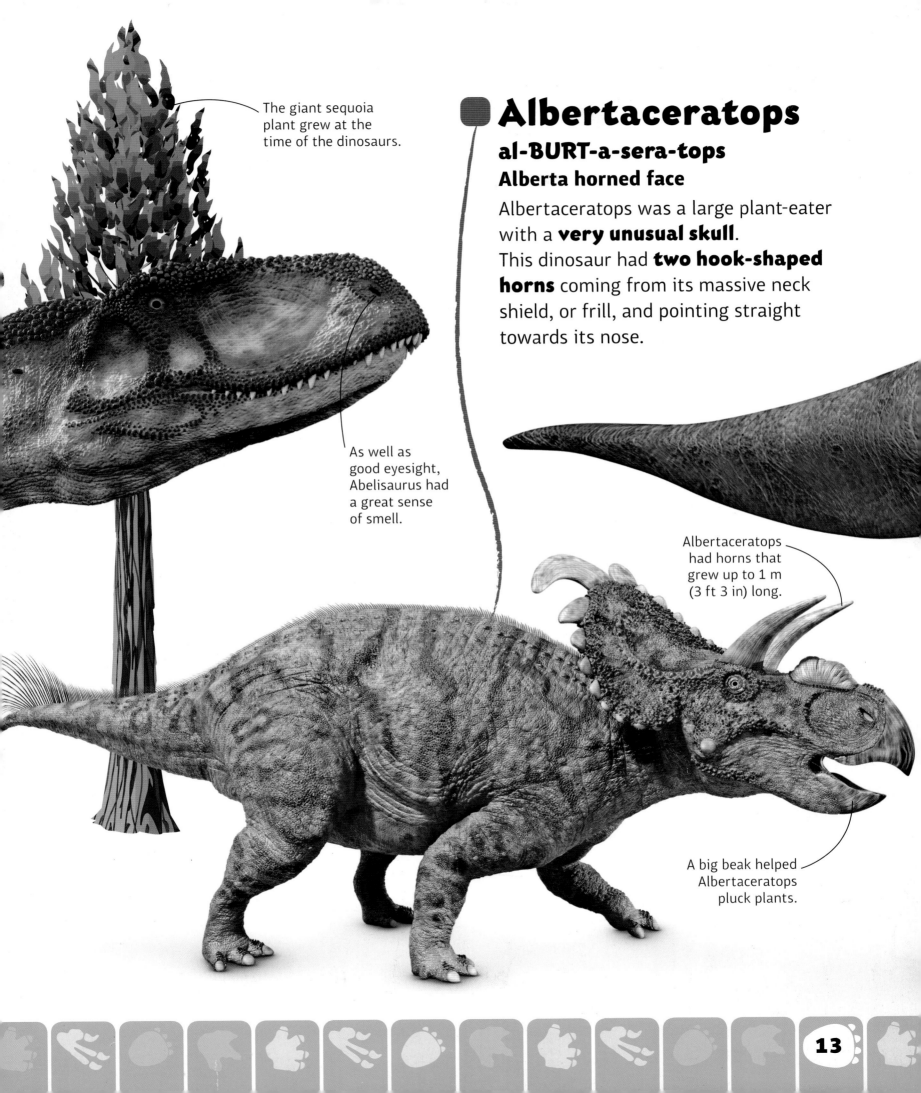

The giant sequoia plant grew at the time of the dinosaurs.

Albertaceratops

al-BURT-a-sera-tops
Alberta horned face

Albertaceratops was a large plant-eater with a **very unusual skull**.
This dinosaur had **two hook-shaped horns** coming from its massive neck shield, or frill, and pointing straight towards its nose.

As well as good eyesight, Abelisaurus had a great sense of smell.

Albertaceratops had horns that grew up to 1 m (3 ft 3 in) long.

A big beak helped Albertaceratops pluck plants.

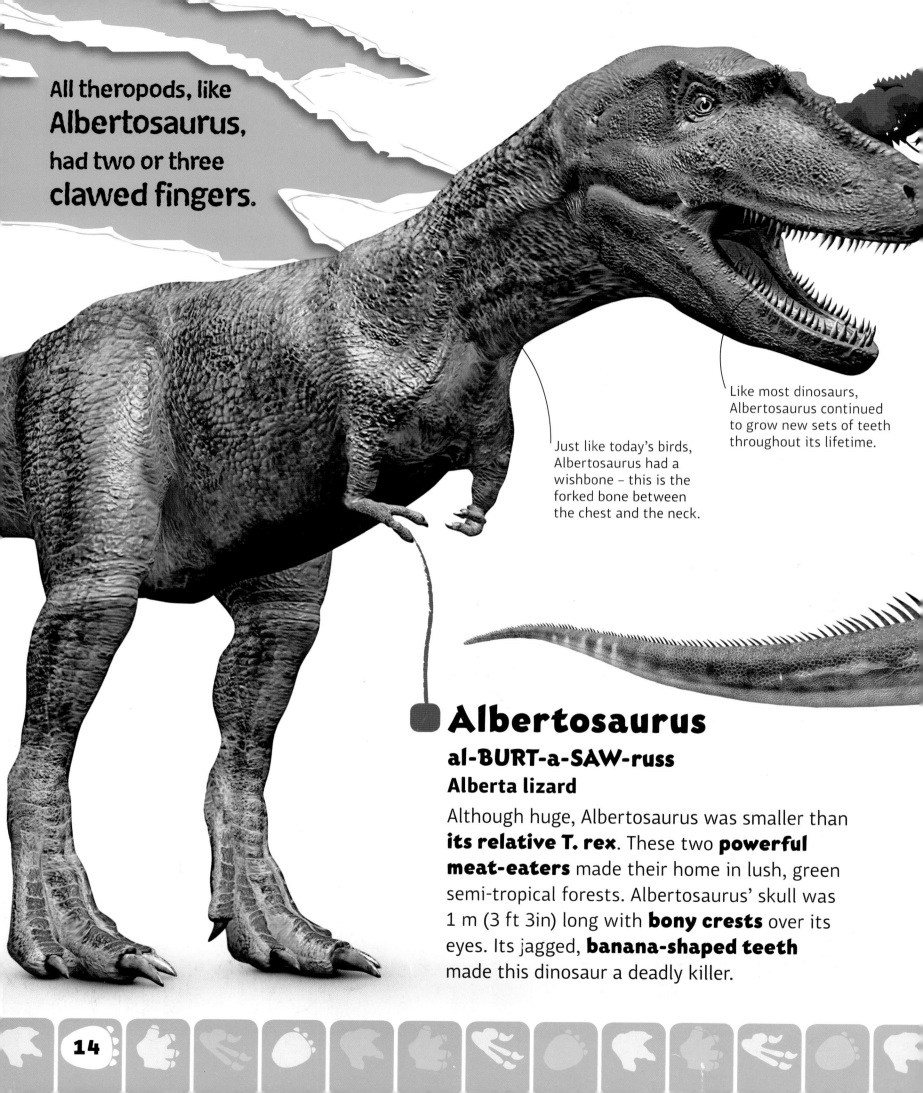

All theropods, like **Albertosaurus**, had two or three **clawed fingers**.

Just like today's birds, Albertosaurus had a wishbone – this is the forked bone between the chest and the neck.

Like most dinosaurs, Albertosaurus continued to grow new sets of teeth throughout its lifetime.

Albertosaurus

al-BURT-a-SAW-russ
Alberta lizard

Although huge, Albertosaurus was smaller than **its relative T. rex**. These two **powerful meat-eaters** made their home in lush, green semi-tropical forests. Albertosaurus' skull was 1 m (3 ft 3in) long with **bony crests** over its eyes. Its jagged, **banana-shaped teeth** made this dinosaur a deadly killer.

Trees first grew about 380 million years ago.

The Mesozoic Era is considered the "Age of Dinosaurs". This period lasted from about 250 million to 65 million years ago.

Allosaurus
alloh-SAW-russ
Different lizard

Allosaurus was a meat-eating dinosaur with **rows of large, sharp teeth**. When it closed its jaws, Allosaurus' teeth acted like blades to slice through bone. Dinosaur experts have found so many Allosaurus remains that we know it was one of the **greatest predators** of the Jurassic Period.

Strong jaws helped Allosaurus capture and hold on to prey.

Many theropods were fast-moving meat-eaters who chased down their prey.

Sauropods had the **longest tails** of any animal to have **ever lived** on Earth.

Amargasaurus
a-MAR-ga-SAW-russ
La Amarga lizard

Amargasaurus was a small sauropod, with an **odd-looking neck**. A nearly complete skeleton was discovered in La Amarga Arroyo in Argentina. "La Amarga" means "bitter creek". Amargasaurus had two rows of spines that ran from its head along the top of its neck and down its shoulders. This dinosaur didn't have teeth, so swallowed the plants it ate whole.

Spines and spikes were very rare among dinosaurs with long necks.

Amargasaurus, like all sauropods, walked on four legs.

Anchiornis

AN-kye-OR-niss
Near bird

This small dinosaur from the late Jurassic Period had large wings and **feet covered entirely with feathers**. In 2010, paleontologists (dinosaur experts) were able to work out the colour of Anchiornis' feathers. Its body was mostly black and grey, with some **red tufts** sitting on top of its head.

This close-up shows Anchiornis' feathery red tufts.

Ankylosaurus

an-KYE-lo-SAW-russ
Fused lizard

Covered nearly head to toe in **plates and spikes**, Ankylosaurus is the most famous of the **armoured dinosaurs**. These plant-eaters were like walking tanks. They **moved slowly** searching for food while using their incredible armour for defence.

Compared to their bodies, all sauropods had very tiny heads.

Bony plates, called osteoderms, were covered in horn and helped protect Ankylosaurus.

Ankylosaurus used its tail club to defend itself and its young against attack.

Williamsonia was a fern-like plant.

Fossil finds

Dinosaur fossils are rocky copies of dinosaur skeletons. When dinosaurs died, some got buried under layers of mud. Gradually, the bones got replaced by rock, or became fossilized. The fossils tell us what dinosaurs looked like.

Titanosaur had a very small head compared to the rest of its body.

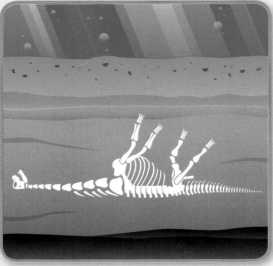

Getting buried

Dinosaurs die from sickness, injury, or old age. This one is lying in mud at the bottom of a lake. Slowly, its body will rot.

Turning to rock

The dinosaur gradually gets covered in mud and sand. Its flesh rots away, leaving only bones behind. Over millions of years, the bones turn to rock.

Digging it up

A dinosaur expert, called a palaeontologist, discovers the fossilized remains of the dinosaur. She carefully digs up the dinosaur.

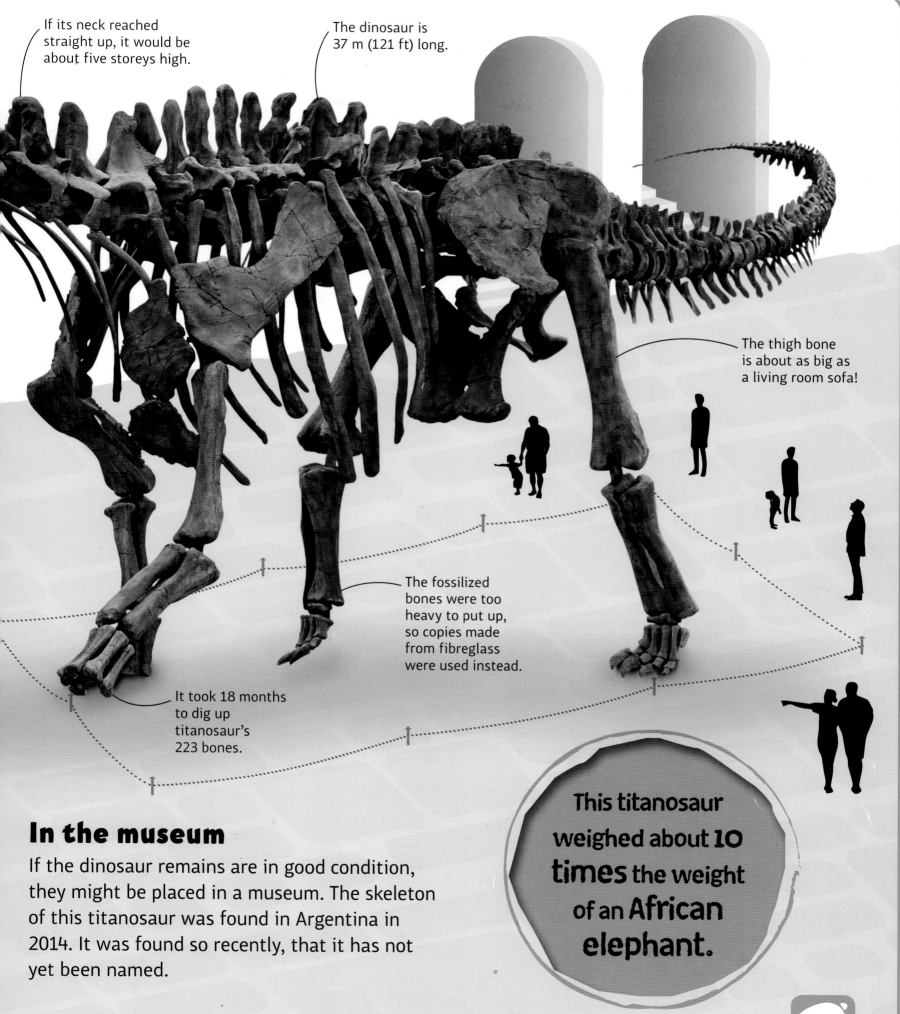

If its neck reached straight up, it would be about five storeys high.

The dinosaur is 37 m (121 ft) long.

The thigh bone is about as big as a living room sofa!

The fossilized bones were too heavy to put up, so copies made from fibreglass were used instead.

It took 18 months to dig up titanosaur's 223 bones.

In the museum

If the dinosaur remains are in good condition, they might be placed in a museum. The skeleton of this titanosaur was found in Argentina in 2014. It was found so recently, that it has not yet been named.

This titanosaur weighed about 10 **times** the weight of an **African elephant.**

Sauropod tails contained lots of bones called vertebrae.

Tall, seed-producing plants, like this ginkgo, were a tasty snack for many plant-eating dinosaurs.

Soft ground such as mud or sand are ideal for leaving **footprints** that may later **fossilize**.

Like Apatosaurus, many sauropods had toe claws!

Incredibly long tails could be used like a whip to scare away dinosaurs.

Sauropods had the longest necks of any animal group.

Do Apatosaurus and Brontosaurus belong to the **same group?** Scientists are still arguing about this.

This sauropod had massive leg bones and strong muscles to support its huge body.

Apatosaurus
a-PAT-oh-SAW-russ
Deceptive lizard

Apatosaurus was a huge sauropod. It had a small head in proportion to its size. It was also in possession of **a long, whip-like tail**. Apatosaurus had **pencil-like teeth** with worn-down tips. It used these to scrape greenery off branches.

Light and hollow neck bones made it easier for Apatosaurus to raise its head to the top of trees to feed.

Large ferns, like Tempskya, grew in warm, wet areas during dinosaur times.

As well as being able to fly, Archaeopteryx would probably have been able to run and jump.

Archaeopteryx

AHR-kee-OP-ter-iks

Ancient wing

This bird-like dinosaur could fly, but only short distances. It is very important as it links **dinosaurs** that could not fly with today's **flying birds**.

Dinosaurs probably produced a lot of gas after they had eaten their food!

Argentinosaurus would have left footprints more than 1.5 m (5 ft) long.

This plant, called the Cycadeoidea, is in the fern family.

Argentinosaurus

ahr-jen-TEEN-oh-SAW-russ

Argentine lizard

Giant, long-necked dinosaurs like Argentinosaurus had enormous appetites. They ate **masses and masses** of plants every day. Like most sauropods, Argentinosaurus was an expert in stripping the leaves from the highest branches of tall trees.

Sharp claws helped Austroraptor grab other dinosaurs to eat.

Argentinosaurus is among the **largest** dinosaurs to have ever lived.

Argentinosaurus chopped up plants in its jaws before swallowing.

Its long tail helped Barosaurus balance and turn sharply while being chased.

Austroraptor had a long, skinny skull, with many smooth, cone-shaped teeth.

Austroraptor

OW-stroh-RAP-tor

Southern seizer

Austroraptor was **discovered in Argentina**. It belonged to a family of **feathered dinosaurs**, called dromaeosaurs. It is one of the largest of the **dromaeosaurs**.

Giant
Sequoia tree

Barosaurus
BA-row-SAW-russ
Heavy lizard

This North American **plant-eater** used its long neck to reach the highest treetops. Barosaurus was absolutely massive. It ate constantly to keep its huge body well fed.

We know a lot about Barosaurus' limbs and spine, but its feet and skull remain a mystery, as they are yet to be discovered.

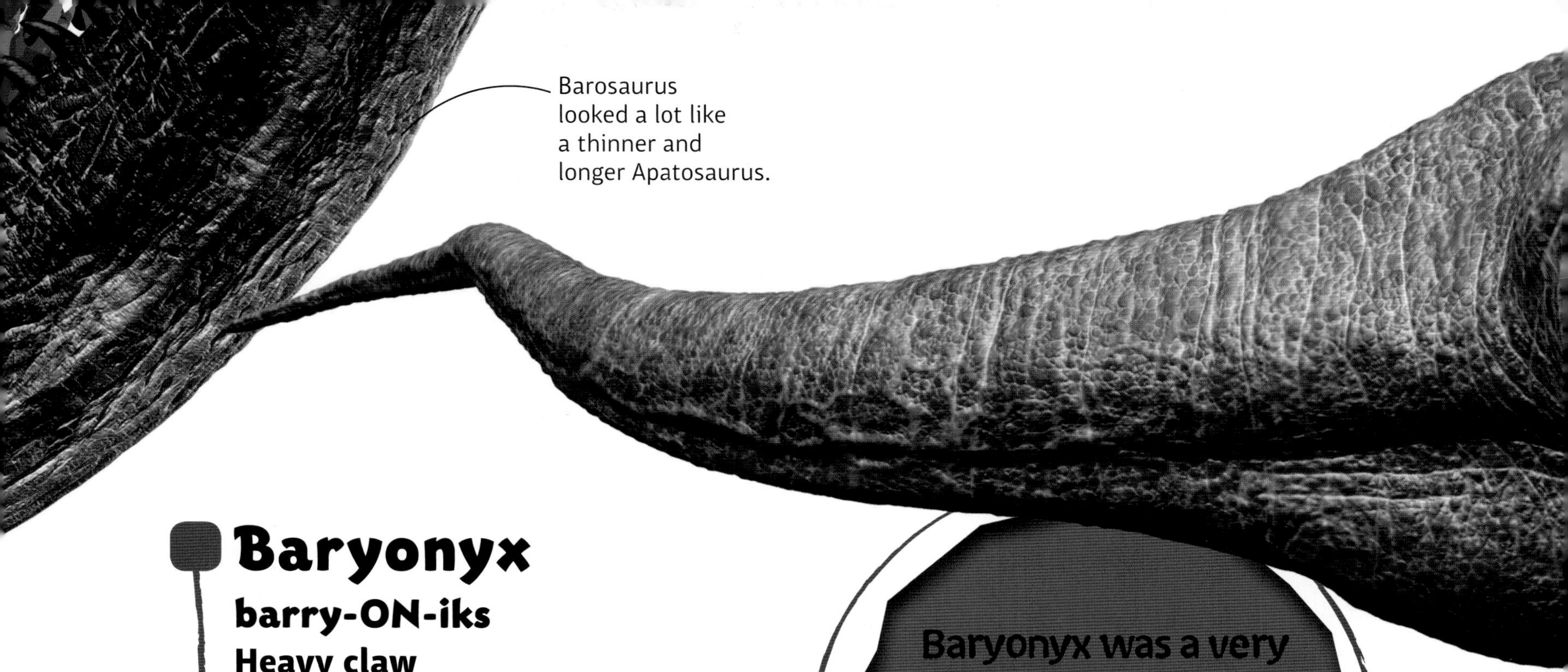

Barosaurus looked a lot like a thinner and longer Apatosaurus.

Baryonyx

barry-ON-iks

Heavy claw

Baryonyx was a **hunter** with **giant claws** and a long, narrow jaw. Living in western Europe, this dinosaur was probably a **fish-eater** that occasionally feasted on smaller dinosaurs and pterosaurs.

Baryonyx was a very clever hunter. It used its claws to catch fish in lakes and rivers.

Baryonyx had lots and lots of small teeth – nearly twice as many as T-rex!

Strong arms were used to help capture fish.

Dinosaurs had great **senses** of **sight** and **hearing.**

The Williamsonia plant grew all over the world at the time of the dinosaurs.

Brachiosaurus had a large crest above its eyes.

Brachiosaurus

brak-KEY-oh-SAW-russ
Arm lizard

This sauropod dinosaur was one of **the largest animals** to ever walk the face of the Earth. Its front legs were longer than its back legs, so its **neck went upwards like a giraffe's**. This probably allowed Brachiosaurus to feed from the **highest trees**.

This dinosaur walked on huge powerful legs.

Brachiosaurus' feet were nearly 1 m (3 ft 3 in) long!

Tall conifer
trees grew in
many places.

The bones towards the end of a dinosaur's tail are called chevrons.

Brachylophosaurus,
like most hadrosaurs,
cared for their young
in groups.

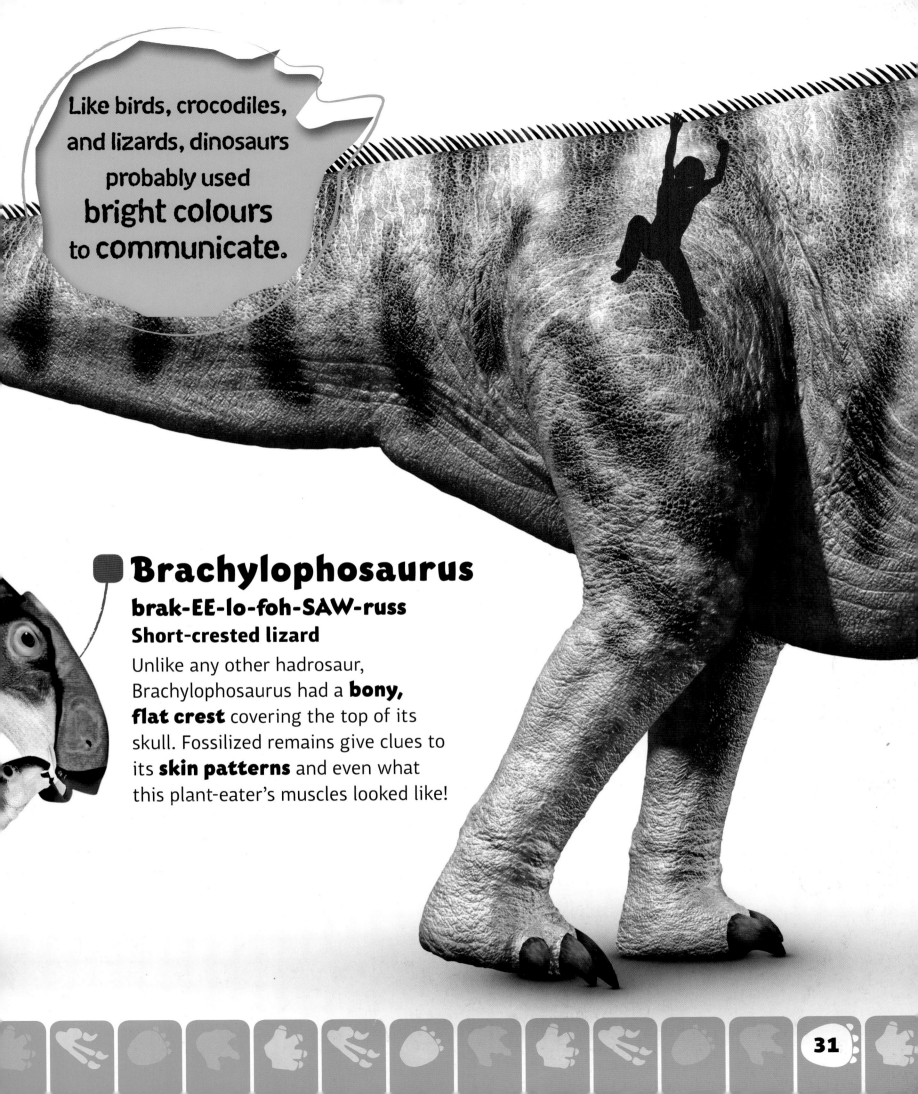

Like birds, crocodiles, and lizards, dinosaurs probably used **bright colours** to **communicate.**

Brachylophosaurus

brak-EE-lo-foh-SAW-russ
Short-crested lizard

Unlike any other hadrosaur, Brachylophosaurus had a **bony, flat crest** covering the top of its skull. Fossilized remains give clues to its **skin patterns** and even what this plant-eater's muscles looked like!

Araucarioxylon could grow to be 60 m (197 ft) tall and was one of the sauropods' favourite foods.

Sauropods, like Camarasaurus, needed a very strong heart to pump blood all the way from their chest to their head.

Camarasaurus

KAM-ar-oh-SAW-russ
Chambered lizard

Many brilliant Camarasaurus **body fossils** have been found. The tracks they left behind tell us they **travelled in groups**. Camarasaurus had a **square-shaped skull**, and was probably hunted by Allosaurus.

Some sauropods, like Camarasaurus, had leg bones that were bigger than an adult human!

Camptosaurus

kamp-TOE-SAW-russ

Flexible lizard

Camptosaurus was **quite small** compared to the rest of its beaked relatives. It was very **strong and quite heavy** though, which helped protect it from being attacked. These plant-eaters lived in North America and were some of the first dinosaurs **ever discovered**.

Nostrils were far enough away from the mouth to stop plants tickling the dinosaur's nose while eating.

There is a **nearly complete** skeleton of Camptosaurus at the American Museum of Natural History in New York City, USA.

Camptosaurus had very big cheeks to help it hold and eat more plants.

Its tail helped Camptosaurus balance while running.

Strong, sturdy legs helped Camptosaurus run fast and escape attack.

Tempskya was a tree-like fern.

Dinosaur homes

During the time of the dinosaurs, the Earth's climate was warmer than today. This resulted in a wide variety of plants and habitats. Herbivores would gather to feed on the plants. Wherever there were herbivores, there would also be carnivores hunting them!

Riverbank

Riverbanks were rich hunting grounds for dinosaurs. Some fed on fish that swam in the rivers. Others ate ferns and other plants that grew along the water's edge. Small mammals would go to the riverbank to drink, and they became easy prey for any hungry meat-eating dinosaur that passed by.

Iguanodon's beak and teeth were perfect for eating plants.

Ferns

Desert

Some dinosaurs were able to survive in dry habitats. Large desert plants that flowered provided food and water. Dinosaurs weren't the only ones living in these hot, dry places. Small animals, such as scorpions, also scuttled around!

Citipati was a theropod that lived in the Gobi Desert, in China and Mongolia.

Pleuromeia

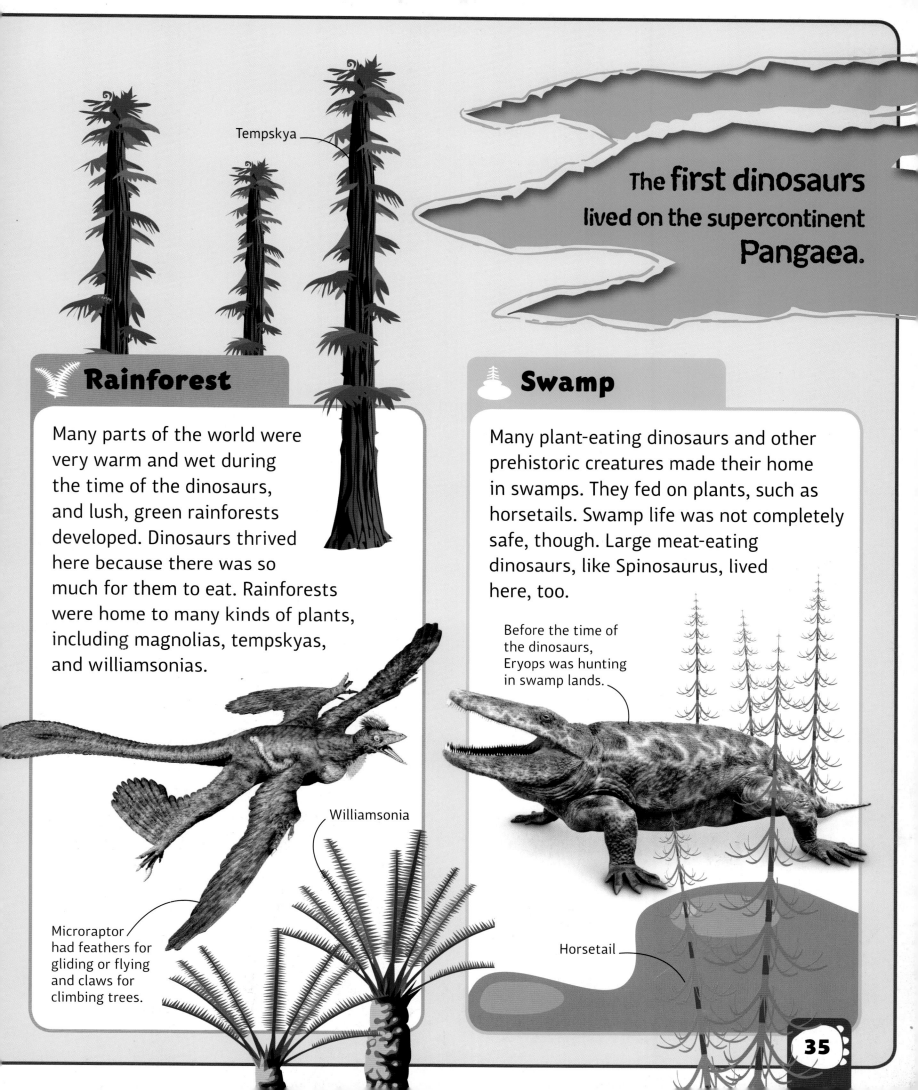

Tempskya

The **first dinosaurs** lived on the supercontinent **Pangaea.**

Rainforest

Many parts of the world were very warm and wet during the time of the dinosaurs, and lush, green rainforests developed. Dinosaurs thrived here because there was so much for them to eat. Rainforests were home to many kinds of plants, including magnolias, tempskyas, and williamsonias.

Williamsonia

Microraptor had feathers for gliding or flying and claws for climbing trees.

Swamp

Many plant-eating dinosaurs and other prehistoric creatures made their home in swamps. They fed on plants, such as horsetails. Swamp life was not completely safe, though. Large meat-eating dinosaurs, like Spinosaurus, lived here, too.

Before the time of the dinosaurs, Eryops was hunting in swamp lands.

Horsetail

Carcharodontosaurus was one of the largest meat-eaters to ever set foot on Earth.

Massive legs may have helped dinosaurs hold down prey.

Huge conifers, such as this Sequoia, provided a tasty meal for Carcharodontosaurus' plant-eating prey!

Carcharodontosaurus had one of the largest skulls of any land animal that ever lived.

Carcharodontosaurus could swallow small dinosaurs whole with its giant mouth!

Most theropods had sharp claws for grasping prey.

Carcharodontosaurus

Kar-karo-DON-toe-SAW-russ
Shark-toothed lizard

This **powerful meat-eater** had jaws about 1.6 m (5 ft 3 in) in length. They were filled with jagged teeth that grew more than 20 cm (8 in) long. Dinosaur experts believe that Carcharodontosaurus used these powerful tools to **slice into** the muscles of its prey.

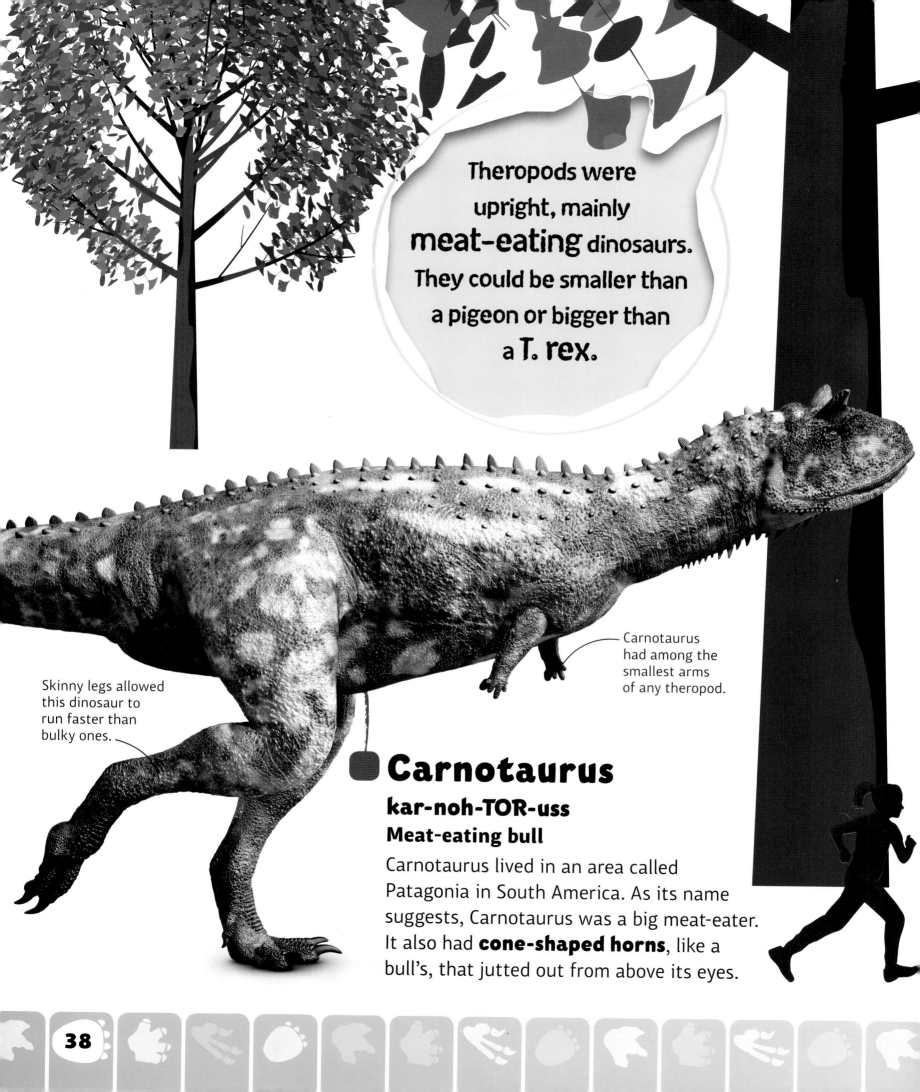

Theropods were upright, mainly **meat-eating** dinosaurs. They could be smaller than a pigeon or bigger than a T. rex.

Carnotaurus had among the smallest arms of any theropod.

Skinny legs allowed this dinosaur to run faster than bulky ones.

Carnotaurus

kar-noh-TOR-uss

Meat-eating bull

Carnotaurus lived in an area called Patagonia in South America. As its name suggests, Carnotaurus was a big meat-eater. It also had **cone-shaped horns**, like a bull's, that jutted out from above its eyes.

The ginkgo plant had fan-shaped leaves.

Centrosaurus
SEN-tro-SAW-russ
Pointed lizard

Centrosaurus is special because it is one of the only ceratopsians with a neck frill that has **spikes pointing forwards**. It may have used its large frill to help **recognize** another Centrosaurus. It may have also used it for **fighting**.

Caudipteryx
kor-DIP-ter-iks
Tail feather

If Caudipteryx was still alive today, it might be mistaken for a **strange bird**. Caudipteryx may have eaten small animals as well as plants. Although it was almost completely feathered, it was **unable to fly**.

It's possible that no two dinosaurs had exactly the same frill.

Ceratosaurus

see-RAT-oh-SAW-russ
Horned lizard

Ceratosaurus was a fairly large theropod with a **blade-like horn** on the top of its snout. This meat-eater had **bony plates** running along the top of its spine. It also had especially **long teeth** in its upper jaw.

Ceratosaurus' remains have been found in the USA and Portugal.

Ceratosaurus had a large triangular shaped horn on its snout.

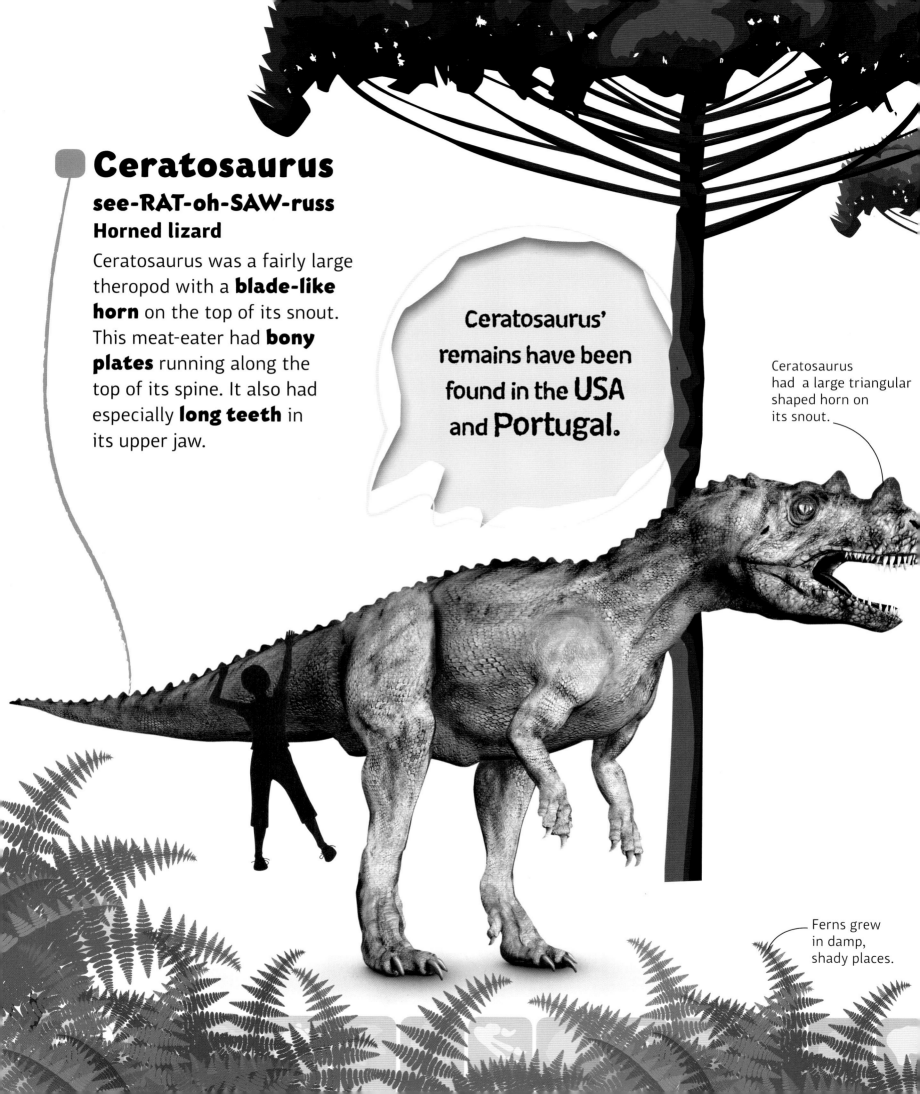

Ferns grew in damp, shady places.

Paraná pine tree

Dinosaurs were the **first** major group of animals to live solely on land.

Citipati

sih-tee-PA-tee
Funeral pyre lord

Citipati was about **the size of an emu**. This dinosaur would sit on top of its **nest of eggs**, protecting them in much the same way as modern birds.

Most small theropods were covered in feathers.

Coelophysis

see-lo-fi-sis
Hollow form

Coelophysis was a small and fast theropod with **great eyesight**. It lived in south-western North America. Remains have been discovered that are so well preserved, we can tell what it had for its **last meal** – a small, **crocodile-like animal** named Hesperosuchus.

Long limbs and hollow bones helped Coelophysis run fast.

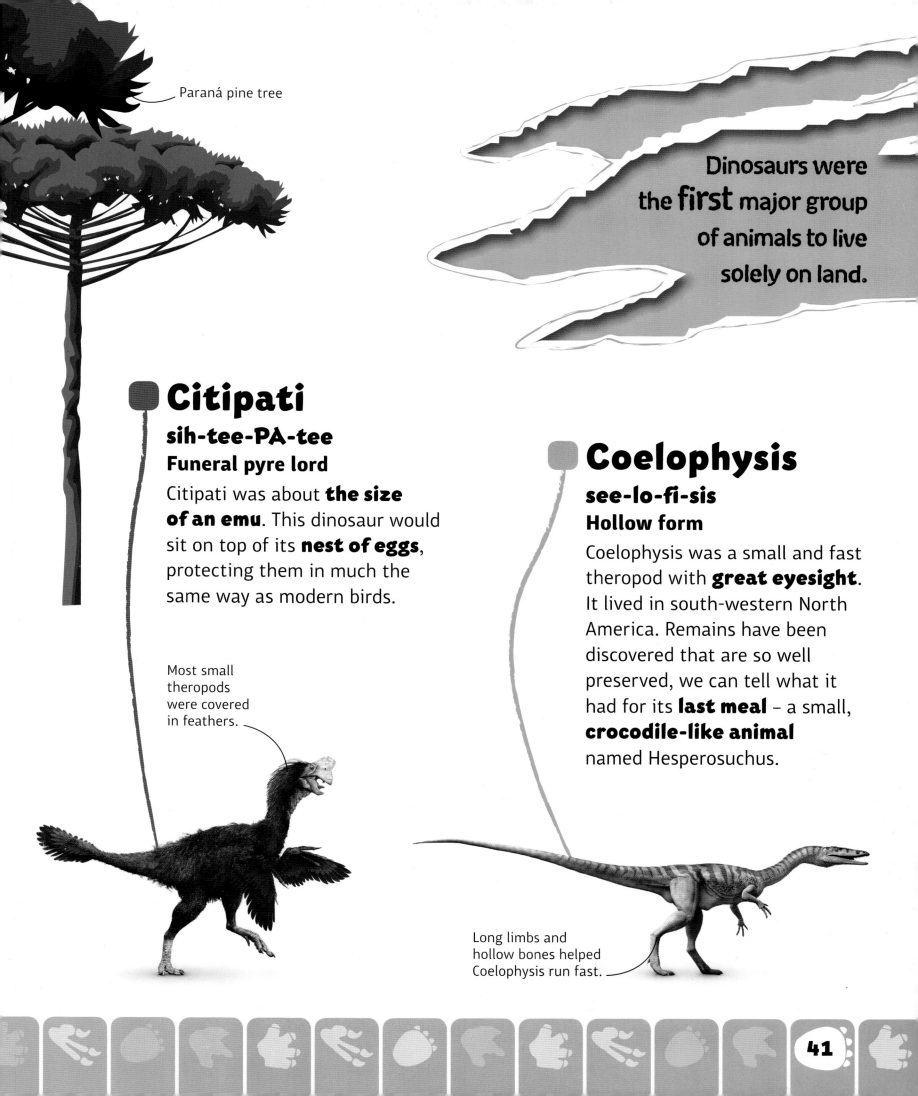

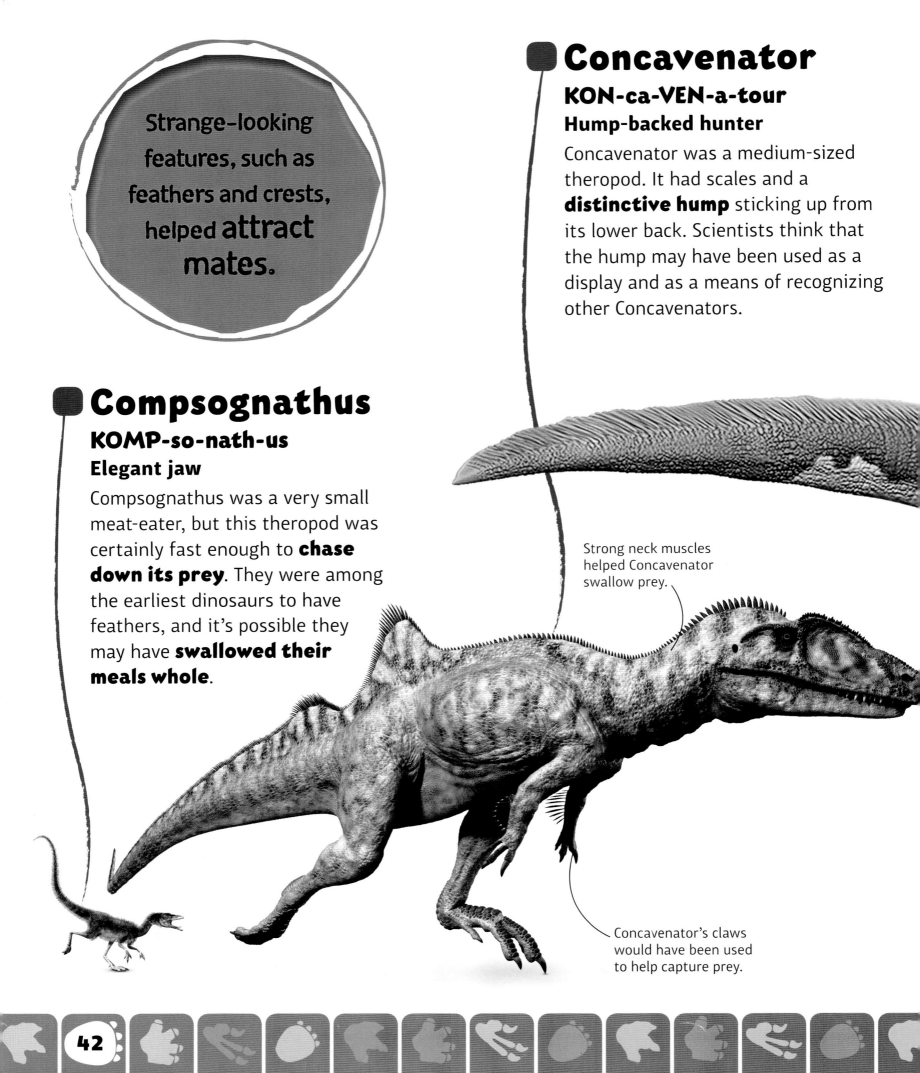

Strange-looking features, such as feathers and crests, helped **attract mates.**

Concavenator
KON-ca-VEN-a-tour
Hump-backed hunter

Concavenator was a medium-sized theropod. It had scales and a **distinctive hump** sticking up from its lower back. Scientists think that the hump may have been used as a display and as a means of recognizing other Concavenators.

Compsognathus
KOMP-so-nath-us
Elegant jaw

Compsognathus was a very small meat-eater, but this theropod was certainly fast enough to **chase down its prey**. They were among the earliest dinosaurs to have feathers, and it's possible they may have **swallowed their meals whole**.

Strong neck muscles helped Concavenator swallow prey.

Concavenator's claws would have been used to help capture prey.

Corythosaurus

cor-ith-o-SAW-russ

Helmet lizard

This duck-billed hadrosaur weighed about 4,000 kg (4 tons) and needed to eat a lot. It had **hundreds of teeth** to help it chew its food. Its **special head crest** was probably used to attract mates or make loud warning calls.

The Sequoia plant grew about 150 million years ago.

Corythosaurus' head crest looked like the helmets worn by ancient Greek soldiers.

The shape of Corythosaurus' front feet suggests it walked on all fours.

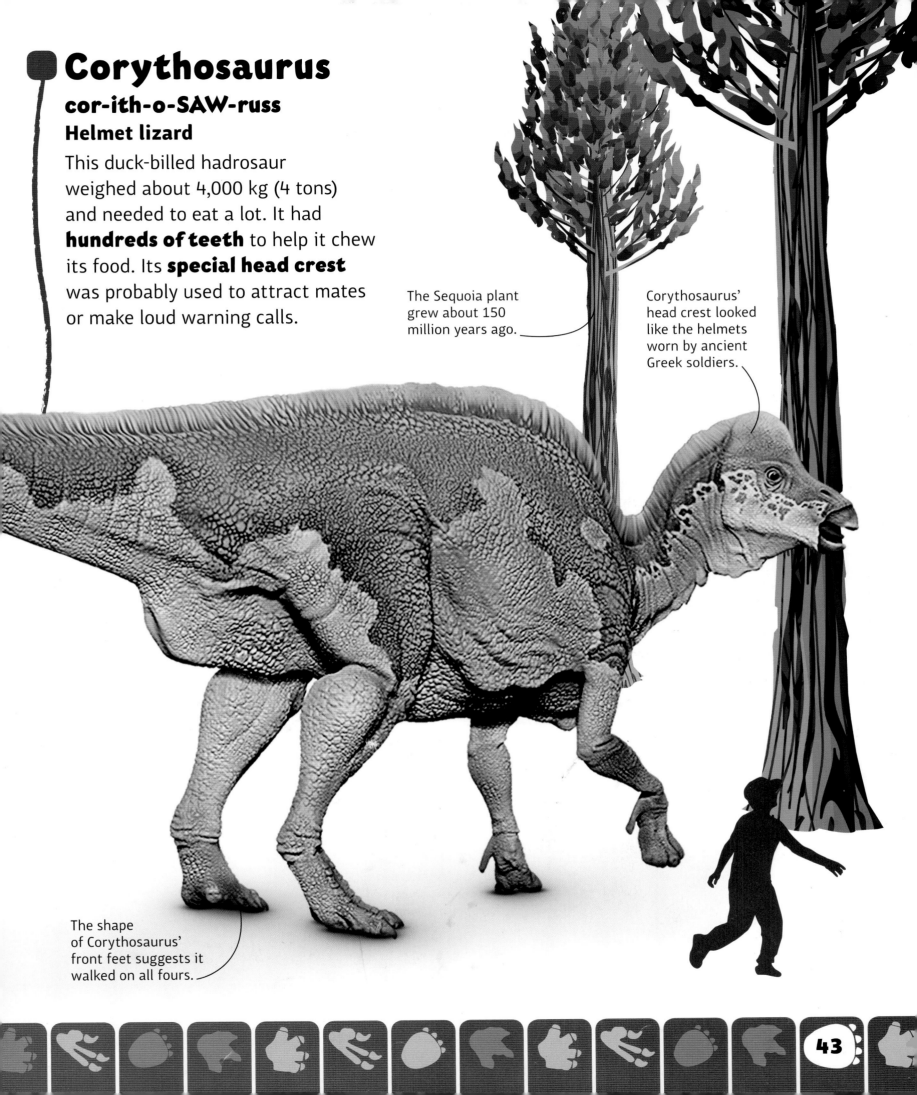

Cryolophosaurus
crya-LOW-foh-SAW-russ
Cold crest lizard

Cryolophosaurus is a unique theropod. It is the only meat-eating dinosaur to have been **found in Antarctica** and is one of the largest theropods of its time. It also had a **horizontal fan** across the top of its narrow forehead.

Most meat-eaters could see in 3D so they were able to focus on their prey very well.

Cryolophosaurus lived in a cooler climate and may have had feathers to keep it warm.

Cryolophosaurus used its powerful legs to run and jump.

The ginkgo plant is still around today.

Daspletosaurus had tail feathers, which may have been used to help attract mates.

Feathers provided warmth. They may also have been **coloured** and used to help select mates.

Long, blade-like teeth would have spelled trouble for nearby dinosaurs.

The end of the tail was covered in large feathers.

While some dinosaurs had **strong jaws** and hundreds of teeth, some species had beaks and mouths with **no teeth!**

Daspletosaurus

das-PLEETO-SAW-russ

Frightful lizard

A medium-sized theropod, this **big meat-eater** lived in western North America. Daspletosaurus had a huge head and **powerful jaws**, which it used to eat dinosaurs such as Centrosaurus and Hypacrosaurus.

Europe

Baryonyx bones that are 125 million years old have been found in England. Compsognathus lived about 150 million years ago in France.

Asia

Protoceratops and Oviraptor lived together about 75 million years ago in Mongolia.

Europe

Compsognathus

Oviraptor

Protoceratops

Asia

Spinosaurus

Africa

Australia

Muttaburrasaurus was first discovered in Queensland, Australia, in 1963.

Muttaburrasaurus

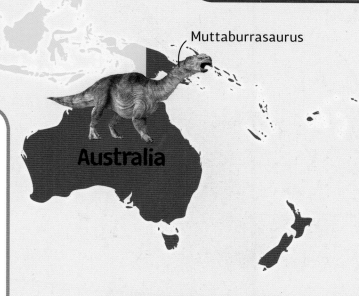

Australia

Africa

Ouranosaurus was first found in the Republic of Niger in 1965. Spinosaurus lived 100 million years ago in Egypt.

Antarctica

Cryolophosaurus was the first theropod dinosaur to be found in Antarctica.

Cryolophosaurus

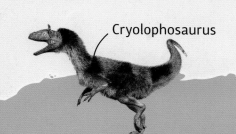

Antarctica

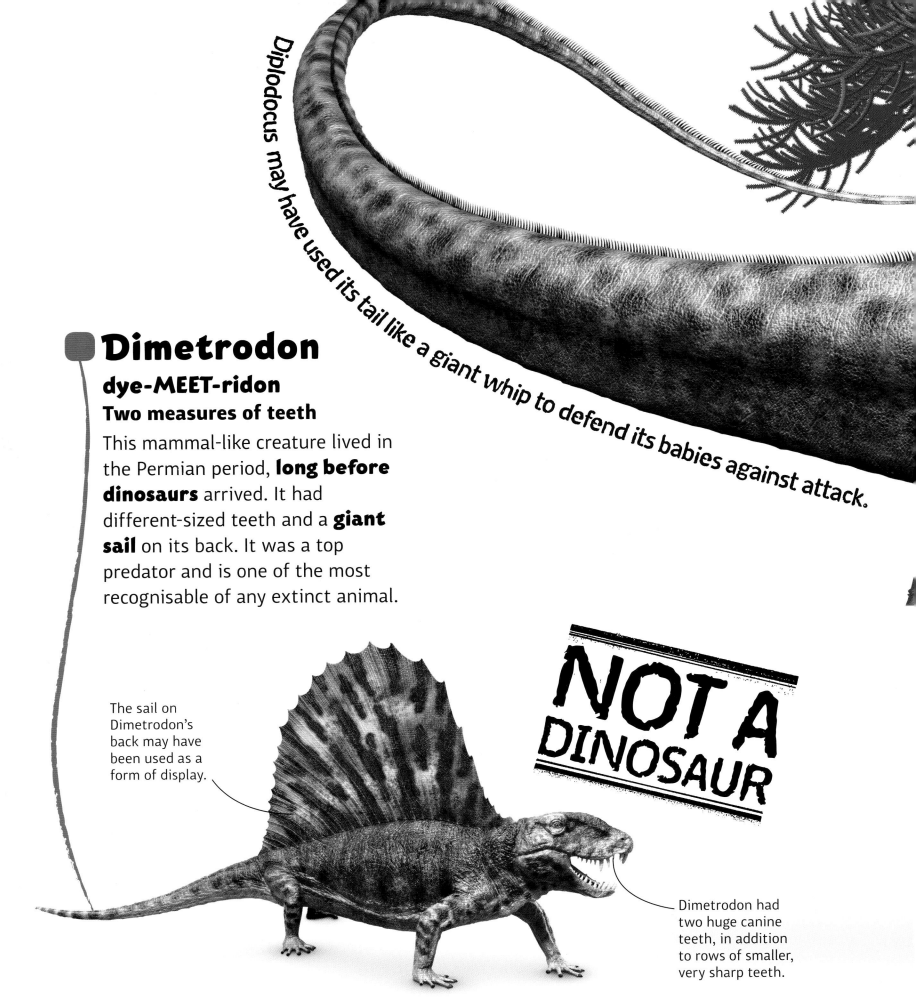

Diplodocus may have used its tail like a giant whip to defend its babies against attack.

Dimetrodon

dye-MEET-ridon

Two measures of teeth

This mammal-like creature lived in the Permian period, **long before dinosaurs** arrived. It had different-sized teeth and a **giant sail** on its back. It was a top predator and is one of the most recognisable of any extinct animal.

The sail on Dimetrodon's back may have been used as a form of display.

NOT A DINOSAUR

Dimetrodon had two huge canine teeth, in addition to rows of smaller, very sharp teeth.

Monkey puzzle, or
Araucaria tree

Diplodocus' legs
were similar to
huge, weight-
bearing pillars.

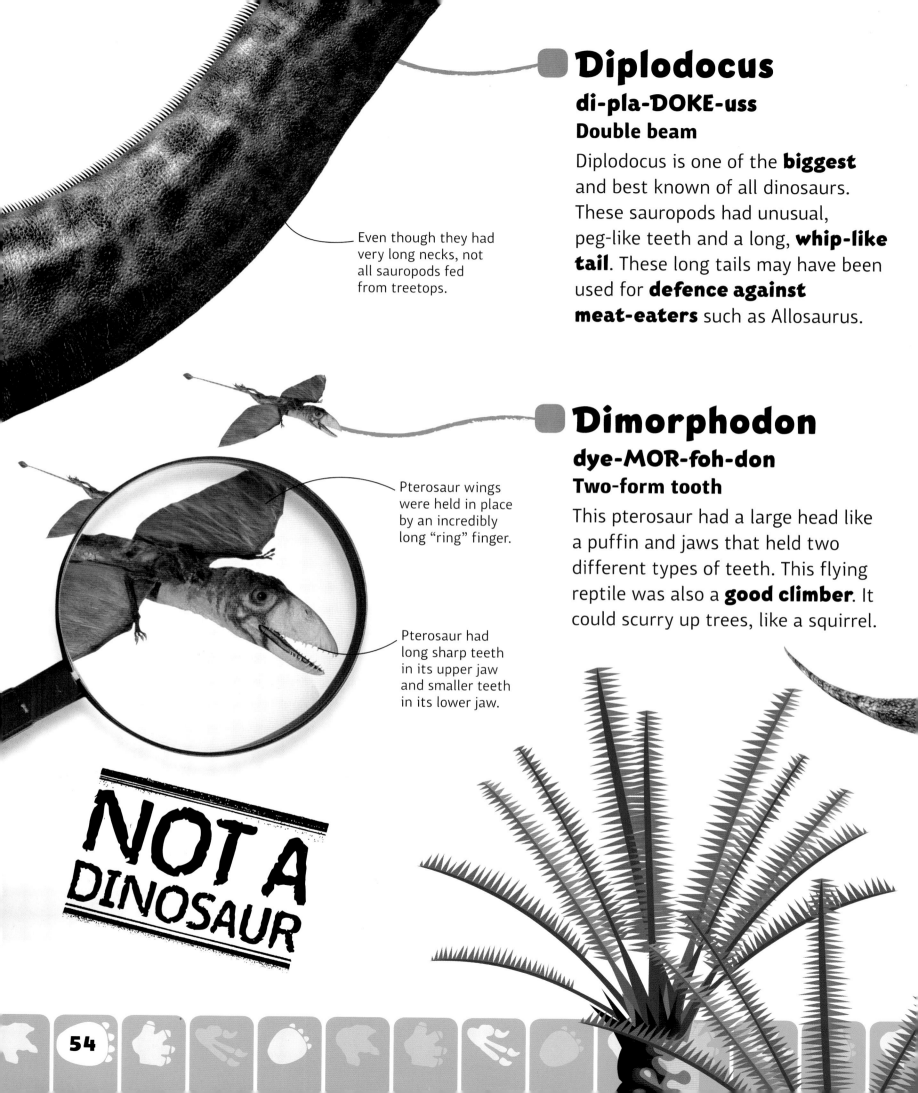

Diplodocus
di-pla-DOKE-uss
Double beam

Diplodocus is one of the **biggest** and best known of all dinosaurs. These sauropods had unusual, peg-like teeth and a long, **whip-like tail**. These long tails may have been used for **defence against meat-eaters** such as Allosaurus.

Even though they had very long necks, not all sauropods fed from treetops.

Dimorphodon
dye-MOR-foh-don
Two-form tooth

This pterosaur had a large head like a puffin and jaws that held two different types of teeth. This flying reptile was also a **good climber**. It could scurry up trees, like a squirrel.

Pterosaur wings were held in place by an incredibly long "ring" finger.

Pterosaur had long sharp teeth in its upper jaw and smaller teeth in its lower jaw.

NOT A DINOSAUR

Although small, Diplodocus' mouth had to take in a lot of food in order to help this giant dinosaur survive.

All dinosaurs had legs that **pointed straight down** from their bodies, not out to the sides, like crocodiles.

The Williamsonia plant had a thick trunk and fern-like leaves.

Dryosaurus
DRY-oh-SAW-russ
Tree lizard

Dryosaurus was an average-sized ornithopod from the late Jurassic period. This plant-eating dinosaur was a **quick runner** with strong legs. It grazed on flat areas of land near rivers, called floodplains, which were green and fertile.

Remains of Dryosaurus have been found in western USA.

Edmontosaurus

ed-MON-toe-SAW-russ

Edmonton lizard

Edmontosaurus had a **very long skull**, which could measure more than a metre (3 ft 3 in) in length. A big skull meant it could have a big mouth with **hundreds of teeth** arranged in long rows. These teeth were continuously being worn down and replaced throughout its life.

Edmontosaurus moved its **lower jaw backwards and forwards** when chewing food.

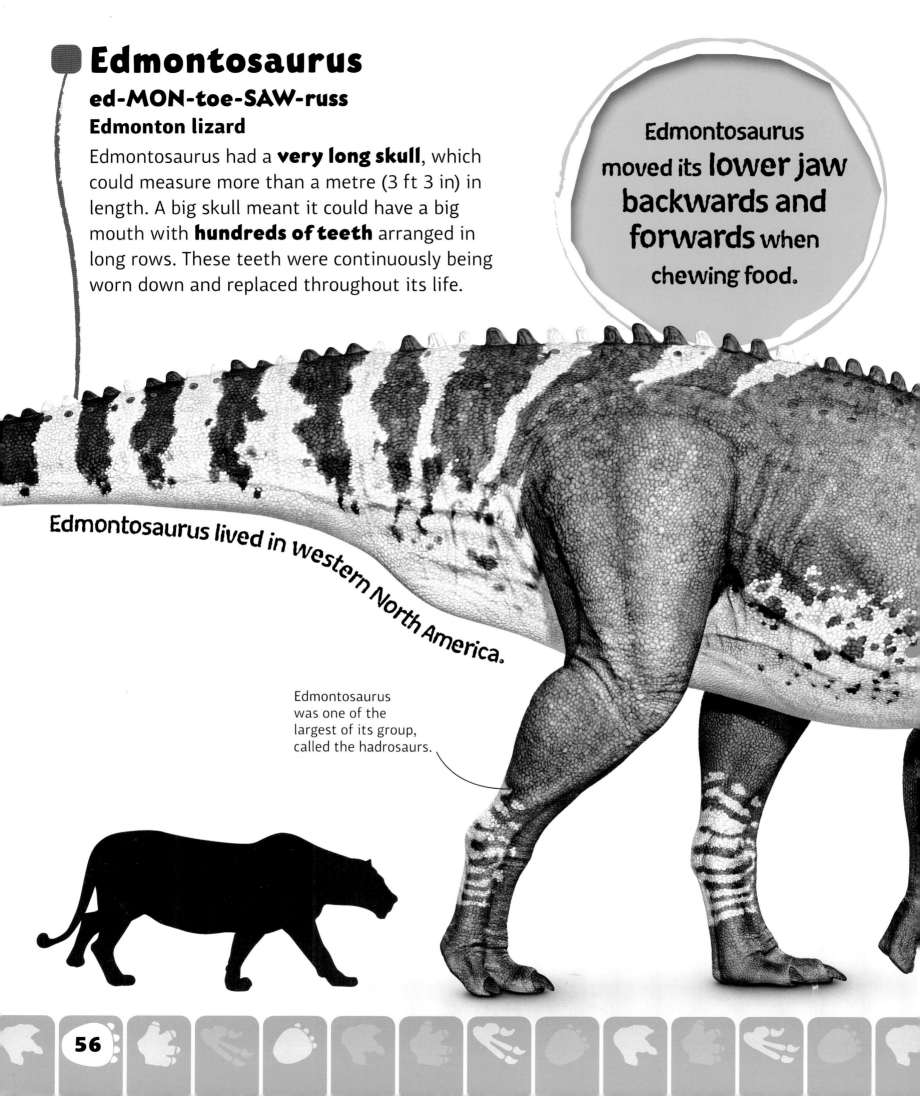

Edmontosaurus lived in western North America.

Edmontosaurus was one of the largest of its group, called the hadrosaurs.

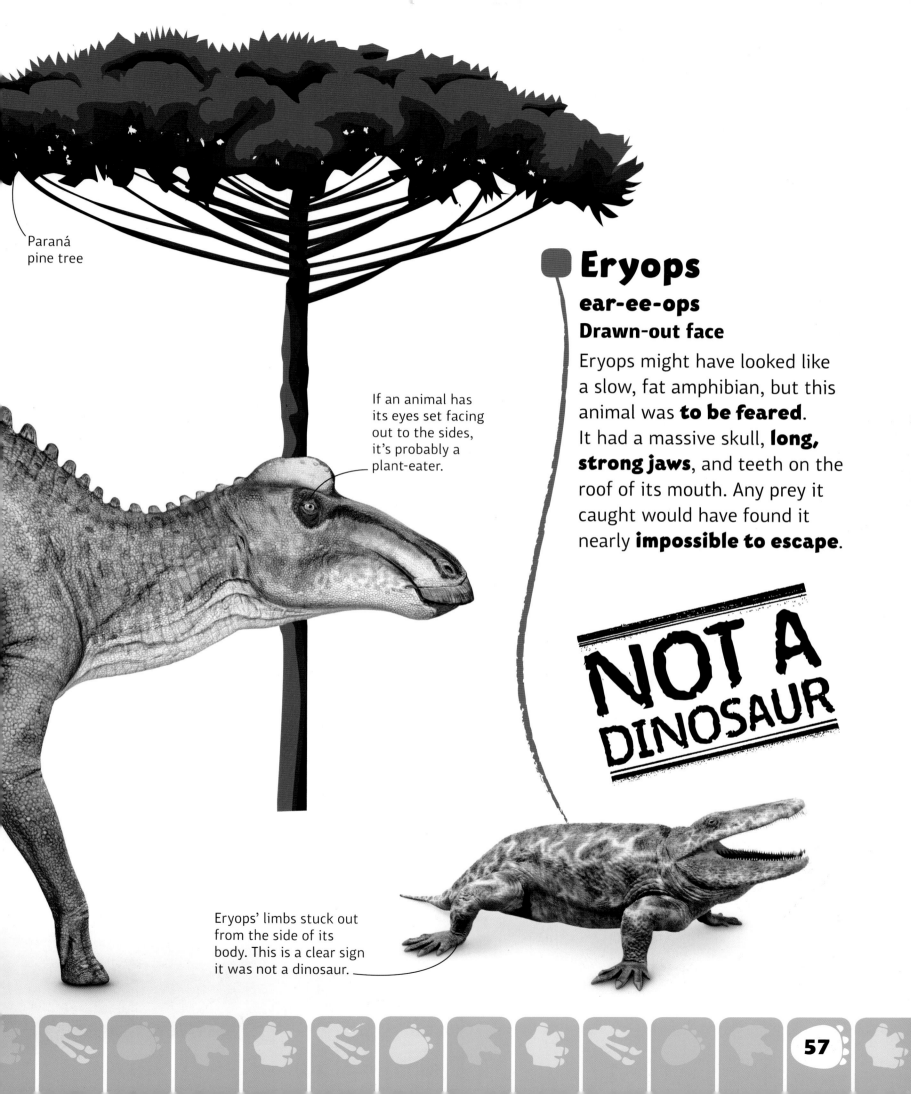

Paraná pine tree

If an animal has its eyes set facing out to the sides, it's probably a plant-eater.

Eryops
ear-ee-ops
Drawn-out face

Eryops might have looked like a slow, fat amphibian, but this animal was **to be feared**. It had a massive skull, **long, strong jaws**, and teeth on the roof of its mouth. Any prey it caught would have found it nearly **impossible to escape**.

NOT A DINOSAUR

Eryops' limbs stuck out from the side of its body. This is a clear sign it was not a dinosaur.

Ginkgo tree

Plant-eating ankylosaurs were so well-protected with armour, they were like **walking tanks.**

Euoplocephalus
YOU-oh-plo-sef-a-luss
Well-armoured head

Living in late Cretaceous North America, Euoplocephalus had **a low, sturdy body**. It had a horned beak, useful for picking plants. With a **bowling ball-sized tail club**, this ankylosaur was well-protected from **carnivores** (meat-eaters) like Gorgosaurus.

When swung with enough power, the tail club of Euoplocephalus could break bone.

Euoplocephalus was completely covered in bony plates and spikes.

Ornithomimids, including Gallimimus, were probably the **fastest group** of dinosaurs.

Gallimimus was one of the largest ornithomimids, called "bird mimics".

Gallimimus

gal-i-MY-mus
Chicken mimic

Gallimimus was a feather-covered theropod. Having no teeth, **they ate stones** (also known as gastroliths) to help them digest plant matter by grinding it up in their belly. Even with a belly full of rocks, they were **among the fastest dinosaurs**. They could run at speeds of about 65 kph (40 mph).

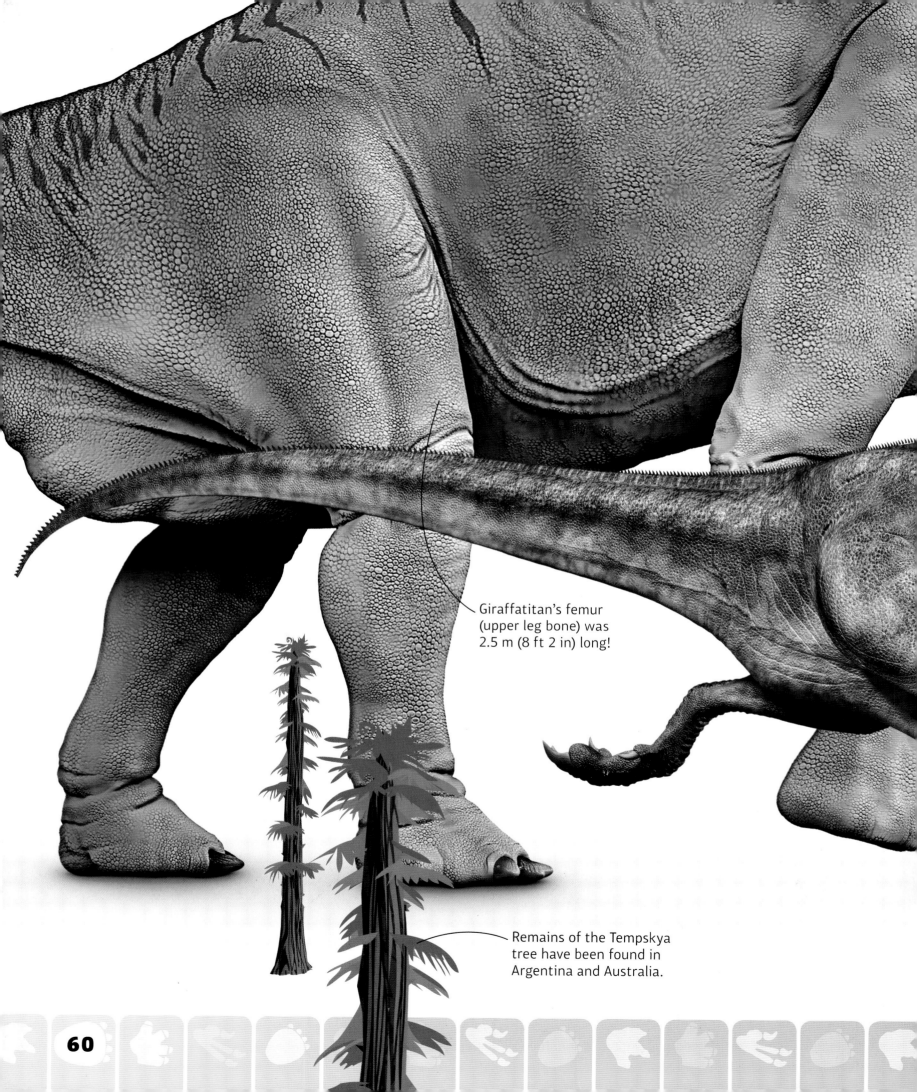

Giraffatitan's femur (upper leg bone) was 2.5 m (8 ft 2 in) long!

Remains of the Tempskya tree have been found in Argentina and Australia.

Giganotosaurus

jig-a-not-o-SAW-russ
Giant lizard

This huge theropod may have been **heavier than T.rex**. It was capable of running about 32 kph (20 mph). This powerful meat-eater was so big it probably even preyed upon some large sauropods!

Some dinosaurs had spines extending from their neck and back.

Giganotosaurus had one of the largest skulls of any animal to ever walk on land.

Massive, powerful claws were used to capture prey.

Gigantoraptor

JIG-an-toe-rap-tor
Giant seizer

Gigantoraptor was more than **twice the height** of an average human. It laid eggs nearly the **size of a rugby ball**. This fearsome meat-eater had hind limbs built for speed, and a **giant, toothless beak**. It would have eaten many small dinosaur species.

The Earth was warmer and wetter during the **Mesozoic Era.** This helped **plants grow** big and tall.

Gigantoraptor looked like a giant chicken. It fed on plants and small animals.

Gigantoraptor's feet would have looked a lot like an emu's.

Scientists can study dinosaur teeth to help work out what type of plants they ate.

Dinosaurs came in all shapes and sizes, from a tiny bird-size to the largest animal to ever walk on land!

Gigantoraptor could use its strong beak to either stab or grab its prey.

Giraffatitan

juh-RAF-ah-TIE-tan
Giant giraffe

For a long time, this giraffe-like giant was believed to be the largest sauropod. These massive plant-eaters had **clawed toes**. They were the **height of a two-storey building** and reached over 20 m (65 ft 7 in) in length. They would have needed to eat about 180 kg (400 lb) of food every single day to survive.

The Cycadeoidea had a short barrel-shaped trunk with a crown of leaves on top.

The strong smell of the leaves of the ginkgo plant may have made dinosaurs want to eat them.

Hadrosaurus

had-ro-SAW-russ
Bulky lizard

Hadrosaurus was the **first dinosaur discovered** in North America. It was also the first to be displayed at a museum, but the **original exhibit was wrong**. It incorrectly showed Hadrosaurus pressing its tail against the ground, similar to the way kangaroos balance.

All duck-billed dinosaurs had beaks.

Herrerasaurus
heh-RARE-ra-SAW-russ
Herrera's lizard

One of the first dinosaurs on Earth, Herrerasaurus was a fast-running meat-eater with **powerful claws** and **sharp teeth**. Herrerasaurus was **fairly small** compared to some of its large theropod relatives. All early dinosaurs were quite small. They grew bigger later in the Mesozoic Era.

Strong hind legs with short thighs and long feet show that Herrerasaurus was a fast runner.

Herrerasaurus had an unusual sliding bottom jaw, which helped it keep hold of its struggling prey.

Rhamphorhynchus
(ram-fo-ring-kus)

Dimorphodon
(dye-MORF-o-don)

Flying reptiles

During the Mesozoic Era, flying reptiles, called pterosaurs, ruled the skies. They also stalked the ground, and could even climb trees in search of prey. They could be as small as a rat or bigger than a giraffe! Pterosaurs were not dinosaurs, but they shared some of the same features. Both were reptiles and both laid eggs.

Microraptor
(MY-crow-RAP-tor)
was actually a
dinosaur, shared
the skies with
pterosaurs!

Pterodactylus
(terra-DACT-aluss)

Pterosaurs
were the first
vertebrates
(animals with a
backbone) to fly.

What pterosaurs ate

Pterosaurs found their food in the sky, in the sea, and on land. These amazing flying survivors were not picky. Their diet included:

- ☑ Fish
- ☑ Molluscs
- ☑ Crabs
- ☑ Insects
- ☑ Dead animals

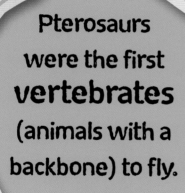

Pterodaustro
(terra-DAW-strow)

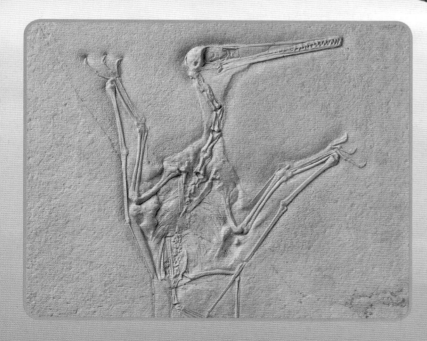

Fossil remains

Pterosaurs had very light, hollow bones so they could fly and glide over great distances. At first, experts thought pterosaurs were sea creatures and used their wings as flippers!

Heterodontosaurus

HET-er-oh-DON-toe-SAW-russ

Different toothed lizard

This small, plant-eater had a narrow skull, a beak, and **three different types of teeth**. Sharp **incisors** at the front of the mouth helped to cut plants. Chisel-like **cheek teeth** helped to break down plants. Large **canine tusks** were probably used for display and possibly fighting.

Hypacrosaurus

hi-PAK-ro-SAW-russ

Near the highest lizard

This plant-eating hadrosaur had a beak shaped like a duck's. It also had a **large, hollow crest** on top of its head. Hypacrosaurus' mouth held hundreds of teeth, and these were continuously being worn down. However, **new teeth continued to grow** and replace old ones during this dinosaur's lifetime.

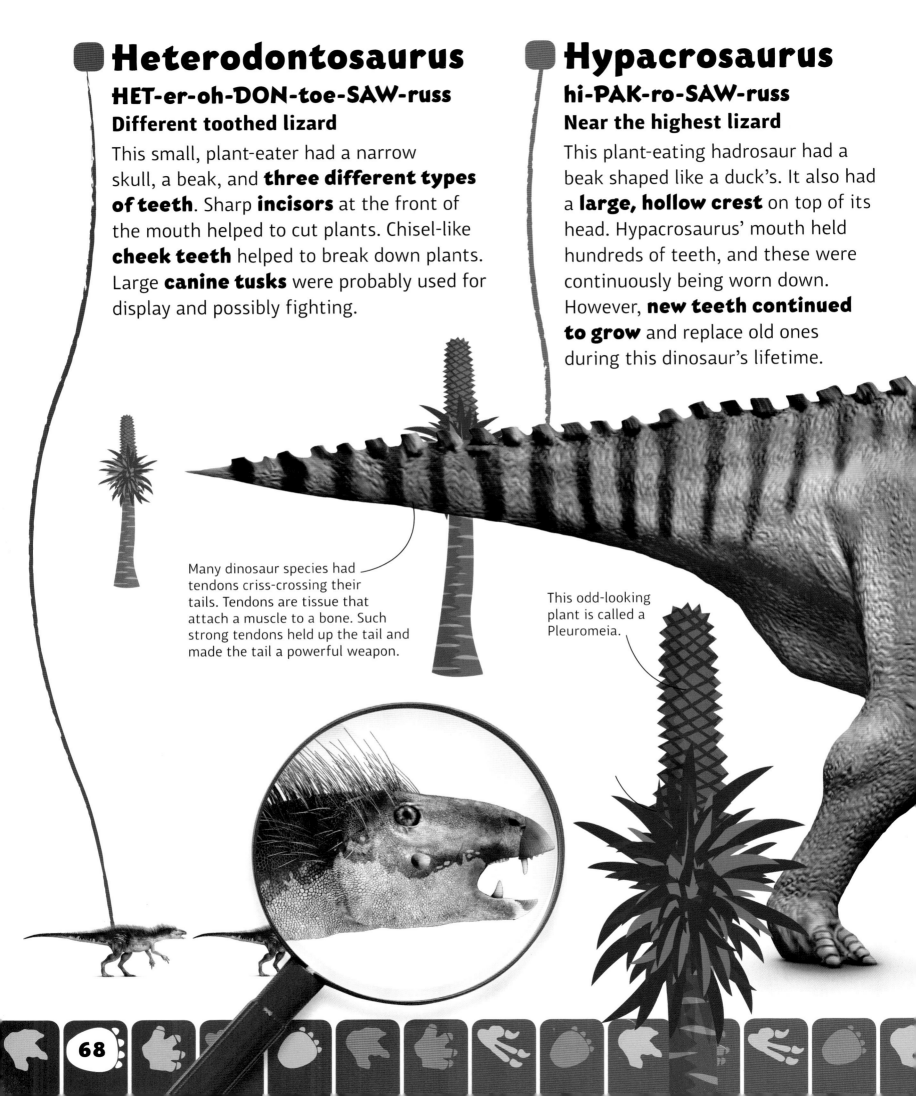

Many dinosaur species had tendons criss-crossing their tails. Tendons are tissue that attach a muscle to a bone. Such strong tendons held up the tail and made the tail a powerful weapon.

This odd-looking plant is called a Pleuromeia.

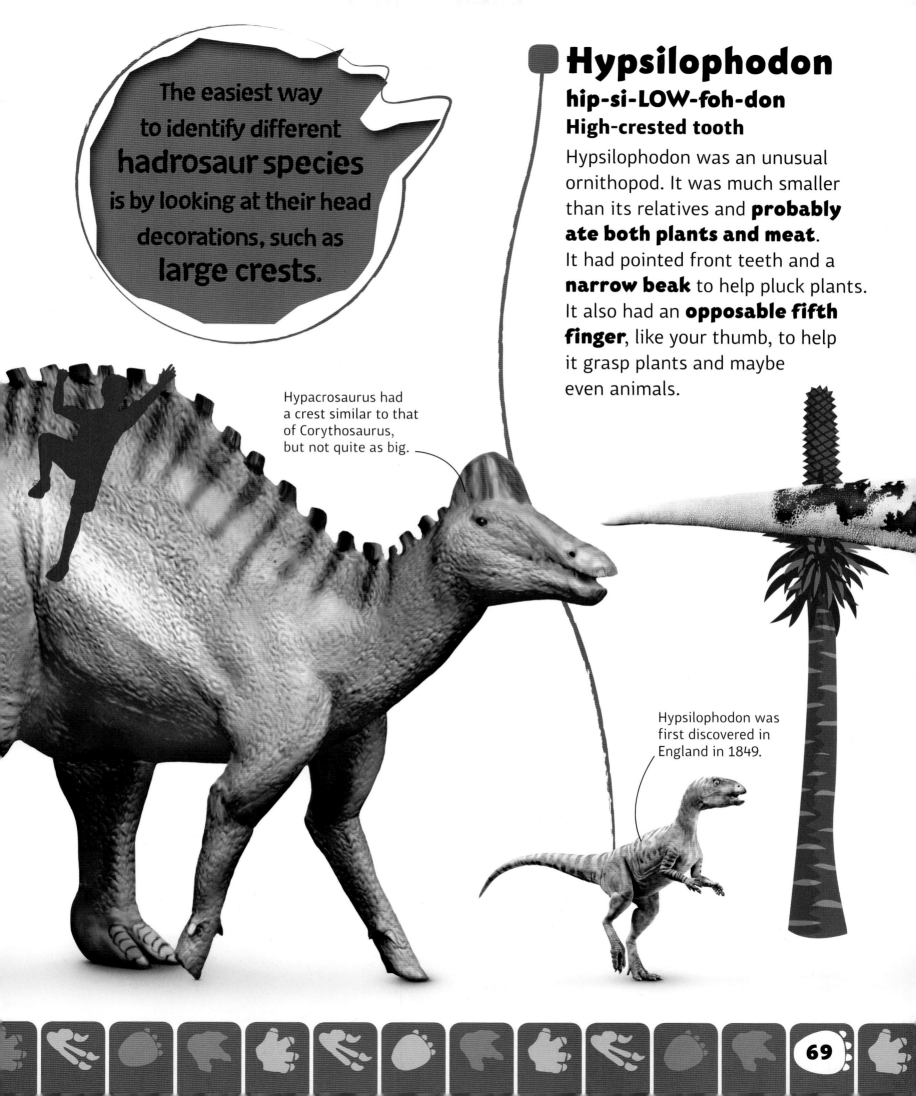

The easiest way to identify different **hadrosaur species** is by looking at their head decorations, such as **large crests.**

Hypsilophodon
hip-si-LOW-foh-don
High-crested tooth

Hypsilophodon was an unusual ornithopod. It was much smaller than its relatives and **probably ate both plants and meat**. It had pointed front teeth and a **narrow beak** to help pluck plants. It also had an **opposable fifth finger**, like your thumb, to help it grasp plants and maybe even animals.

Hypacrosaurus had a crest similar to that of Corythosaurus, but not quite as big.

Hypsilophodon was first discovered in England in 1849.

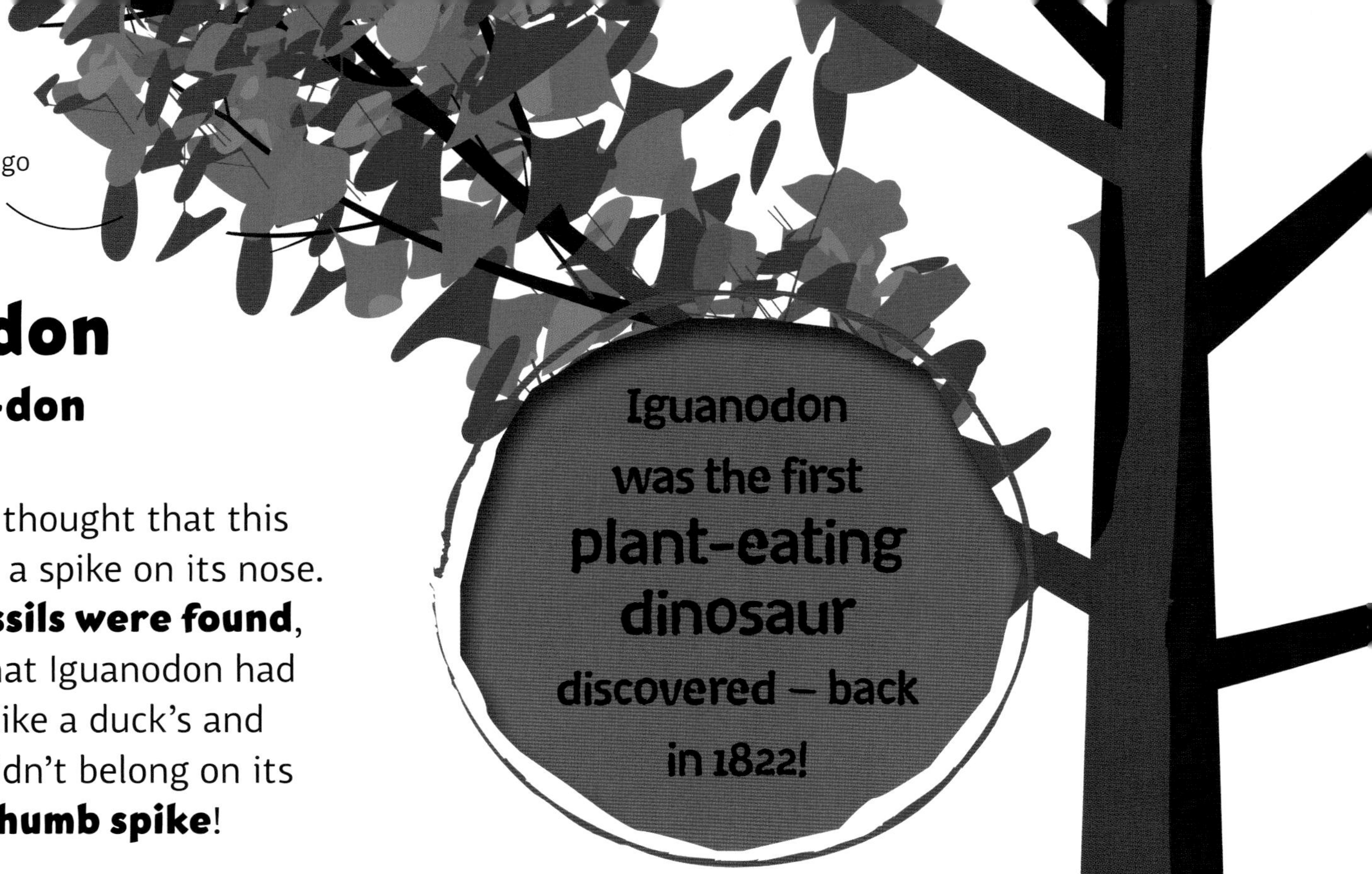

Ginkgo tree

Iguanodon

ig-wahn-oh-don

Iguana tooth

Scientists once thought that this plant-eater had a spike on its nose. After **more fossils were found**, they realized that Iguanodon had a beak shaped like a duck's and that its spike didn't belong on its face. It was **a thumb spike**!

Iguanodon was the first **plant-eating dinosaur** discovered — back in 1822!

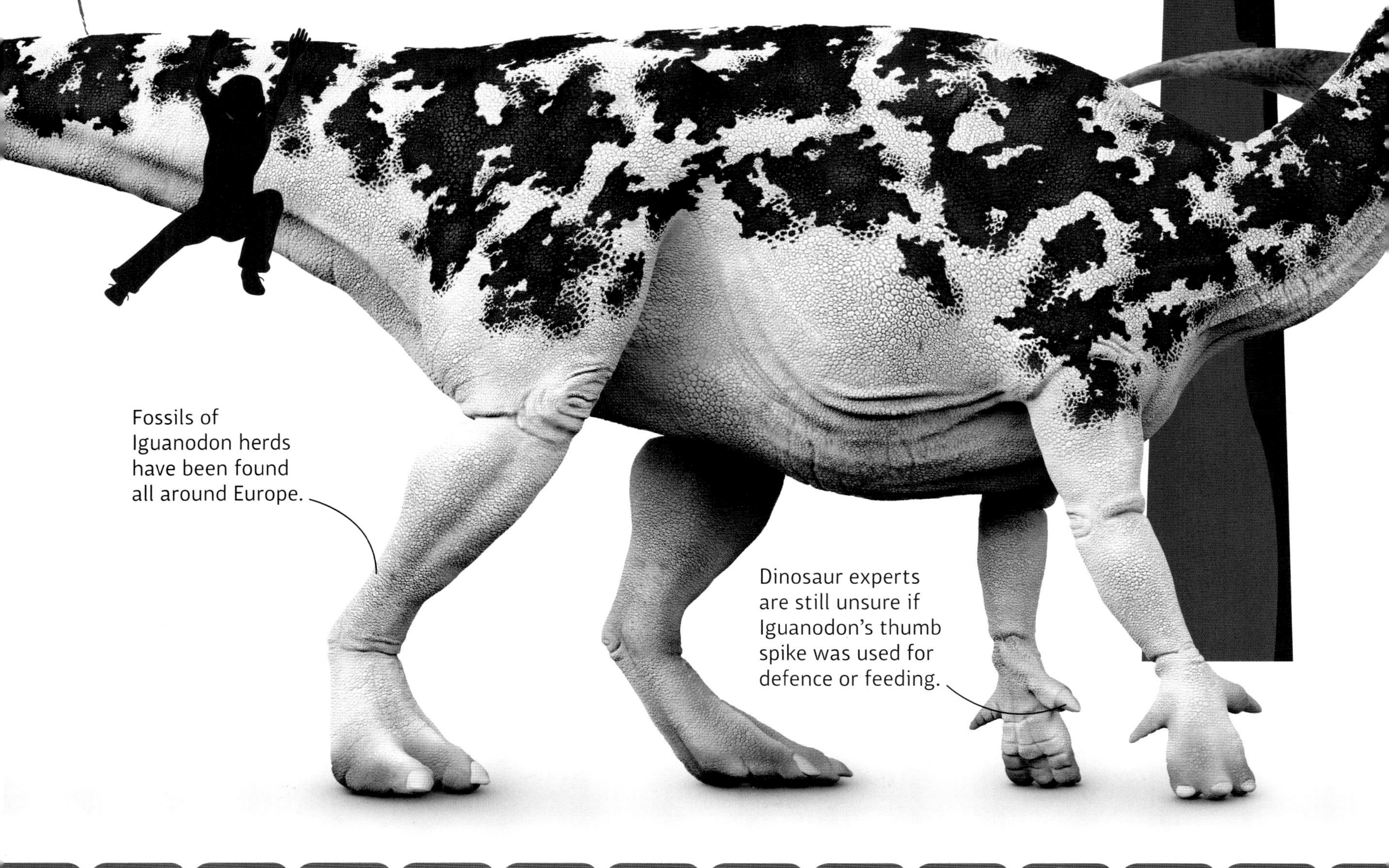

Fossils of Iguanodon herds have been found all around Europe.

Dinosaur experts are still unsure if Iguanodon's thumb spike was used for defence or feeding.

Irritator

IH-ri-tay-tah

Named after the irritation of paleontologists

Irritator was a smaller relative of **Spinosaurus**, but was still fierce. With its **long, narrow jaws** and rows of sharp, cone-shaped teeth, this theropod was a good hunter. It probably spent a lot of time in the water **hunting fish** and other small animals. Its remains were discovered in what is now **Brazil**.

Because its snout looks like an alligator's, dinosaur experts believed Irritator spent a lot of time hunting in rivers, lakes, and streams.

Long, curved claws helped Irritator grasp and hold onto fish.

Not all dinosaurs lived at the same time. Even those that did, might not have met each other.

Studying dinosaurs

Paleontology is the study of ancient life, including dinosaurs and fossils. To be a paleontologist you must be patient and hard-working. Most importantly, you have to be curious. The life you are studying no longer exists, so you must use clues and evidence to piece together puzzles from millions of years ago.

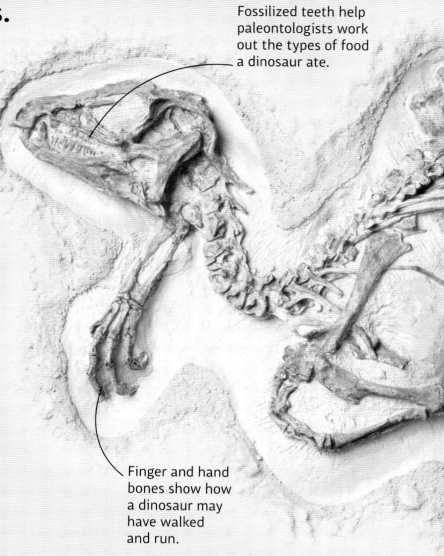

Fossilized teeth help paleontologists work out the types of food a dinosaur ate.

Finger and hand bones show how a dinosaur may have walked and run.

Paleontology

Why is paleontology so important today? By investigating things like fossilized bones, footprints, and eggs, we learn a lot about what life used to be like. It also helps us to understand the world we're living in now and what the future might hold.

Building a dinosaur

It's very rare to find a complete dinosaur skeleton. Often, paleontologists will use the parts of many animals of the same type to piece together a skeleton. Fossilized complete skeletons of smaller dinosaurs are more common than those of large dinosaurs. Sometimes skin texture and feathers can be seen in fossils.

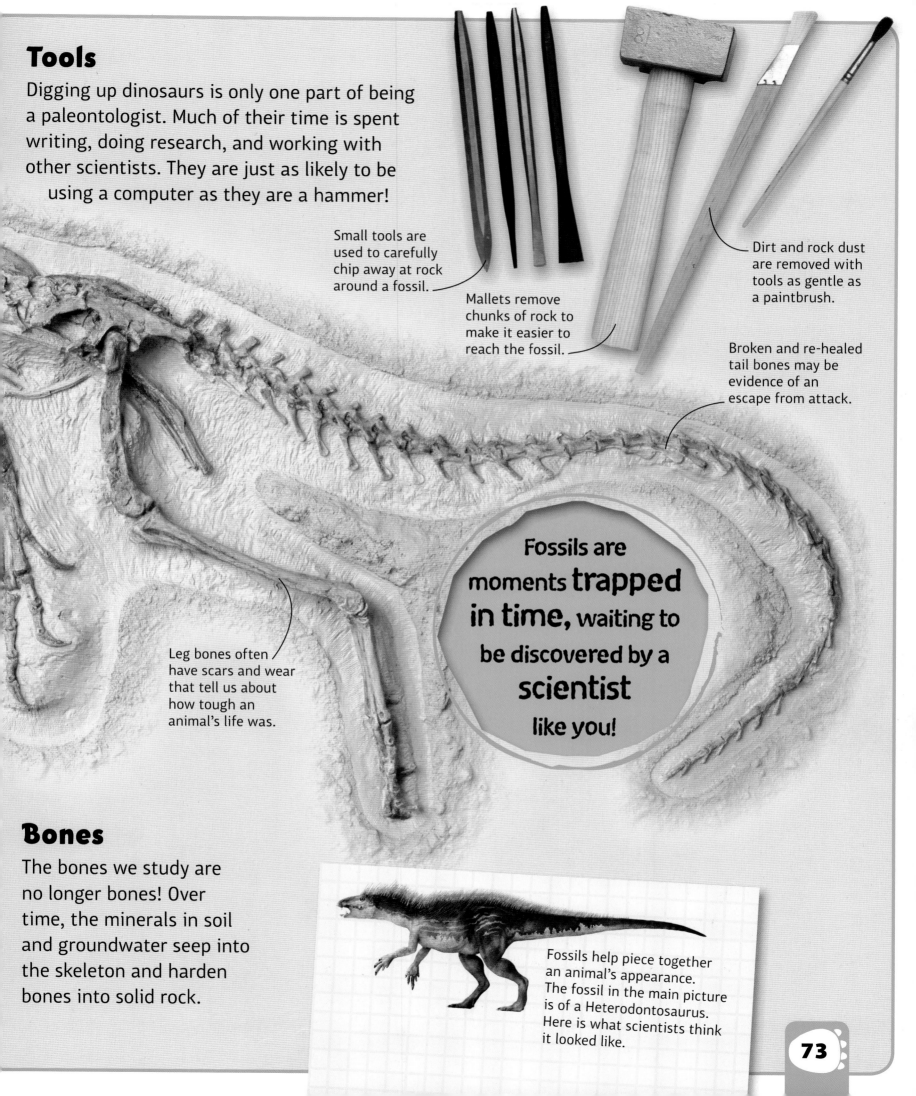

Tools

Digging up dinosaurs is only one part of being a paleontologist. Much of their time is spent writing, doing research, and working with other scientists. They are just as likely to be using a computer as they are a hammer!

Small tools are used to carefully chip away at rock around a fossil.

Mallets remove chunks of rock to make it easier to reach the fossil.

Dirt and rock dust are removed with tools as gentle as a paintbrush.

Broken and re-healed tail bones may be evidence of an escape from attack.

Leg bones often have scars and wear that tell us about how tough an animal's life was.

Fossils are moments **trapped in time,** waiting to be discovered by a **scientist** like you!

Bones

The bones we study are no longer bones! Over time, the minerals in soil and groundwater seep into the skeleton and harden bones into solid rock.

Fossils help piece together an animal's appearance. The fossil in the main picture is of a Heterodontosaurus. Here is what scientists think it looked like.

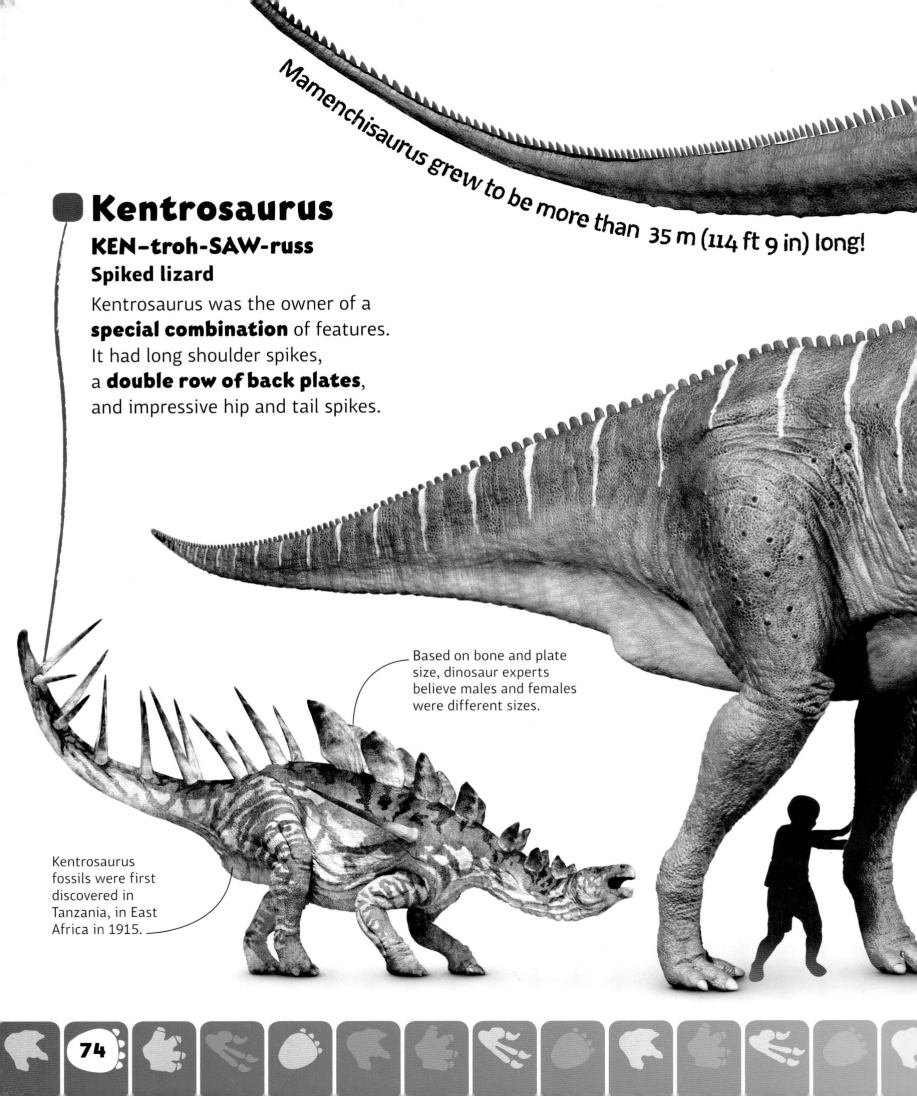

Mamenchisaurus grew to be more than 35 m (114 ft 9 in) long!

Kentrosaurus

KEN–troh–SAW–russ

Spiked lizard

Kentrosaurus was the owner of a **special combination** of features. It had long shoulder spikes, a **double row of back plates**, and impressive hip and tail spikes.

Based on bone and plate size, dinosaur experts believe males and females were different sizes.

Kentrosaurus fossils were first discovered in Tanzania, in East Africa in 1915.

Lambeosaurus would have been able to reach up and feed from the Araucaria tree.

Lambeosaurus had a **unique head crest**. It was the only one with two prongs.

Lambeosaurus
LAM-bee-oh-SAW-russ
Lambe's lizard

This large, plant-eating hadrosaur lived in **western North America** towards the end of the Cretaceous period. Like its close relative, Corythosaurus, Lambeosaurus had a **strange bony structure** on top of its head. It could move on either two legs or four.

At more than 4 m (13 ft) long, Mamenchisaurus had among the largest ribs of all dinosaurs.

Most of the **plants and trees** that grew in the Mesozoic Era are now **extinct**.

Dinosaur **fossils** are often **discovered** at **building sites**. The first Mamenchisaurus remains were found during the **building of a road**!

Maiasaura

my-a-SAW-ra
Good mother lizard

After studying lots of well-preserved remains, dinosaur experts know that Maiasaura travelled in **enormous herds**. It laid lots of eggs at the same time and **cared for its young** in groups. Maiasaura was a plant-eater. It used its **flat beak** to pluck plants.

Like all hadrosaurs, Maiasaura was a plant-eater with hundreds of teeth.

Maiasaura was about 9 m (30 ft) long and probably weighed around 4,000 kg (4 tons).

Large sauropods needed to eat over 1,000 kg (1 ton) of food every single day!

Mamenchisaurus

mah-MEN-chee-SAW-russ
Mamenchi lizard

Mamenchisaurus lived in the late **Jurassic period** in China. It had **an incredibly long neck** that stretched up to 9 m (30 ft)! This **sauropod** was more than 35 m (115 ft) long in total. It weighed about 50,000 kg (55 tons).

Masiakasaurus

MA-she-ka-SAW-russ
Vicious lizard

Masiakasaurus wasn't very large, but this dinosaur's claim to fame was its **amazing set of teeth**. The ones at the front of its mouth **stuck out** instead of pointing up and down. This probably helped it to catch **small prey**.

Williamsonia grew everywhere in the Jurassic Period.

Masiakasaurus was about 2 m (6 ft 6 in) long and lived in Madagascar.

Long feathers on its tail and back legs helped Microraptor glide from tree to tree.

Microraptor was a meat-eater that used two types of serrated teeth to capture and eat animals.

Microraptor
MY-crow-RAP-tor
Small thief or seizer

Microraptor was a small meat-eater that was **covered in feathers**. Even though lots of remains have been found, dinosaur experts are still not sure if Microraptor was a glider, or if it **could use its wings to take off and fly**.

Studying Microraptor has helped scientists understand the relationship between **modern birds** and their **prehistoric ancestors**.

Tempskya

Paraná pine tree

Muttaburrasaurus

mutt-ah-bur-ah-SAW-russ
Reptile from Muttaburra

Muttaburrasaurus is one of the few dinosaurs to have been **found in Australia**. This plant-eater's teeth worked like scissors and were made for **slicing plants**. Scientists are still not sure if it walked on **two or four legs**.

The muzzle on top of Muttaburrasaurus' head was probably used to make special sounds to attract mates.

Like Triceratops, Muttaburrasaurus had teeth for slicing, not grinding.

It's very rare to find the whole skeleton of a large dinosaur. Scientists often use parts from **different dinosaurs** to piece together a complete one.

Neovenator

nee-o-VEN-a-tor

New hunter

Found in southern England, Neovenator is the best known of any **European theropod**. Neovenator was a large, speedy meat-eater with **sharp teeth and good sight**. It was one of the **best hunters** around.

It can take scientists years to work out if a **newly discovered dinosaur** is a new species or belongs to a known dinosaur group.

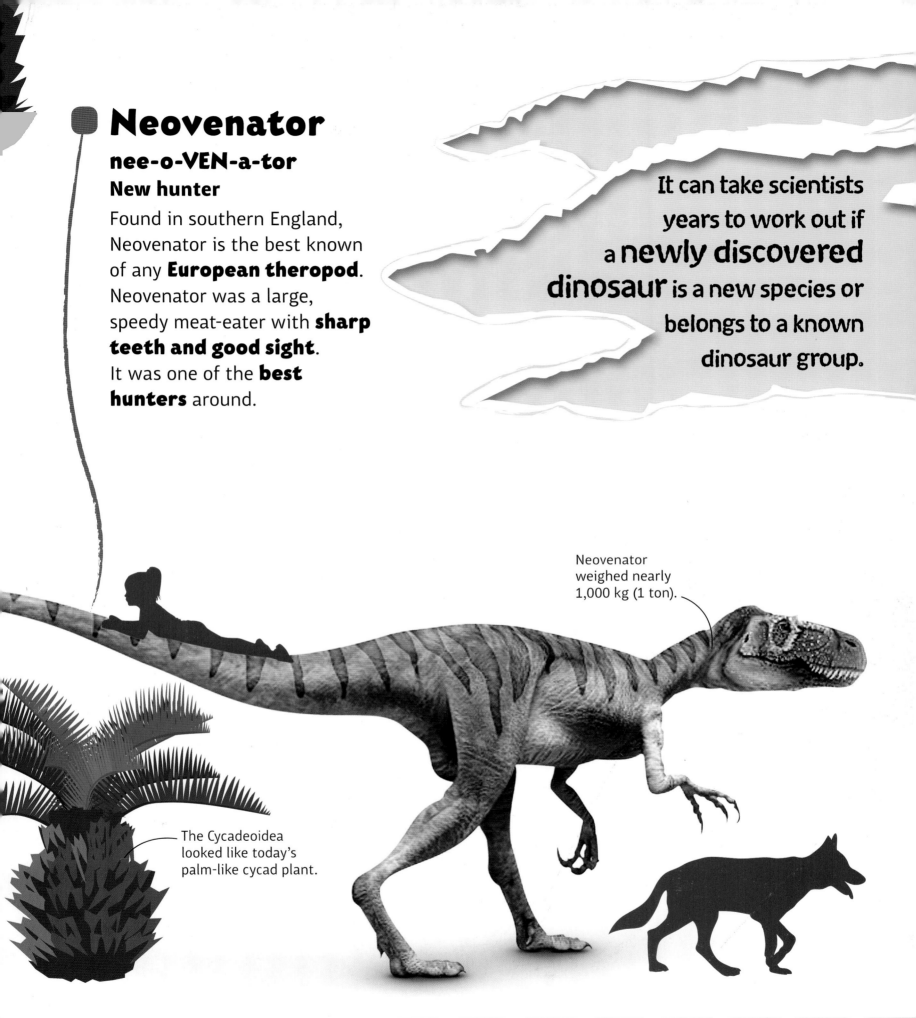

Neovenator weighed nearly 1,000 kg (1 ton).

The Cycadeoidea looked like today's palm-like cycad plant.

Scientists believe Nigersaurus gathered food much **like a lawnmower,** sweeping its neck back and forth while plucking any plants in its path.

Ginkgo tree

Nigersaurus

nee-jur-SAW-russ

Niger reptile

Nigersaurus was a **small sauropod** that lived in what is now the Republic of Niger in Africa, which is how Nigersaurus got its name. Its unique feature was its wide, straight-edged muzzle, or snout. It had a **long row of teeth** running straight across the front of its mouth.

Fossilized **feathers** can provide clues about the **colour** of some dinosaurs.

Nigersaurus' wide, flat muzzle held more than 500 teeth. Each one was replaced every two weeks or so!

Nigersaurus lived about 110 million years ago. It grew to be about 9 m (30 ft) long.

Ornitholestes

or-NITH-oh-less-tees

Bird robber

Ornitholestes was a medium-sized theropod with conical teeth and **small but strong arms**. A speedy runner with terrific eyesight, this dinosaur was a **feared meat-eater** that may have hunted early birds. In fact, Ornitholestes **may itself have had feathers**!

Ornitholestes had the typical S-shaped neck of a theropod.

Creatures of the deep

Millions of years ago, the prehistoric seas and oceans were packed with swimming reptiles. Some, such as Megalodon, were as big as a school bus! Smaller sea creatures swam alongside these extraordinary reptiles. Some of these, such as jellyfish and squid, are still around today.

Mosasaurus
moe-za-SAW-russ
Lizard of the Meuse River

With its huge, sharp teeth and strong tail, giant Mosasaurus was a fierce sea hunter. It is named after the Meuse River, in Europe, where it was first found.

Mosasaurus' jaw could expand, like a snake's, to swallow large prey whole.

Sea turtles first appeared in the mid-Cretaceous period, about 155 million years ago.

Jellyfish have lived in every part of the ocean for more than 500 million years!

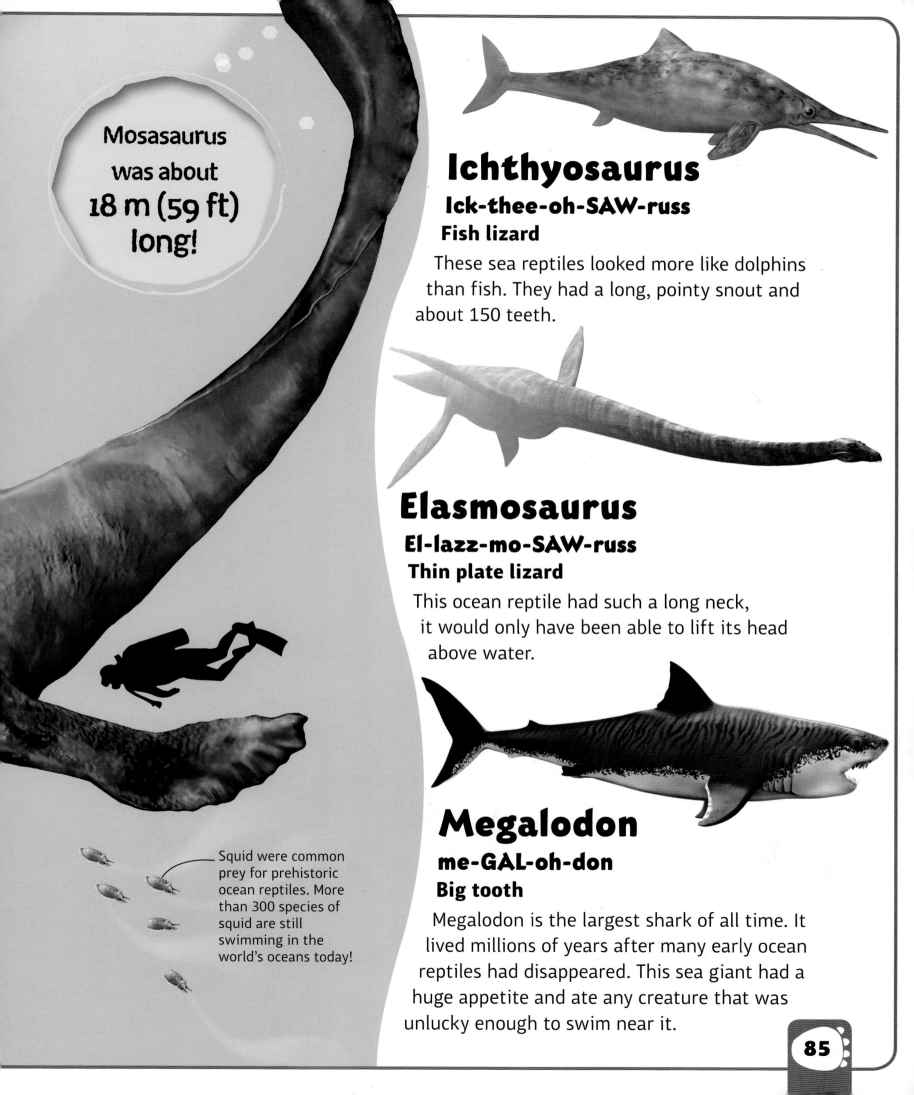

Mosasaurus was about 18 m (59 ft) long!

Ichthyosaurus
Ick-thee-oh-SAW-russ
Fish lizard

These sea reptiles looked more like dolphins than fish. They had a long, pointy snout and about 150 teeth.

Elasmosaurus
El-lazz-mo-SAW-russ
Thin plate lizard

This ocean reptile had such a long neck, it would only have been able to lift its head above water.

Squid were common prey for prehistoric ocean reptiles. More than 300 species of squid are still swimming in the world's oceans today!

Megalodon
me-GAL-oh-don
Big tooth

Megalodon is the largest shark of all time. It lived millions of years after many early ocean reptiles had disappeared. This sea giant had a huge appetite and ate any creature that was unlucky enough to swim near it.

Pachyderm means "thick skin". This is how "Pachyderms", such as elephants, get their name.

Sequoia

Pachycephalosaurus

pak-ee-se-falloh-SAW-russ
Thick-headed lizard

Scientists used to think this plant-eater used its **dome-shaped head crest** in head-to-head combat to try to win mates, like rams do today. They now believe that Pachycephalosaurus could also have used its head **to hit the sides, or flanks,** of other members of its own species, or to **fend off predators**.

Pachycephalosaurus was about 4.5 m (15 ft) long and weighed around 450 kg (990 lb).

Pachycephalosaurus lived at the end of the Cretaceous period, until the extinction of the dinosaurs.

Pachyrhinosaurus

pak-ee-ry-no-SAW-russ
Thick-nosed lizard

Pachyrhinosaurus belonged to a group of plant-eating, beaked dinosaurs called **ceratopsia**. Its remains have only been found in relatively **cold places** such as Alaska and Canada. As well as a massive frill, this plant-eater had a snout that had a huge bony growth on it called a **nasal boss**.

Pachyrhinosaurus skeletons have been found throughout western North America.

Large frills may have added protection.

Nasal boss

Like all ceratopsians, Pachyrhinosaurus was a herbivore with a parrot-like beak.

Williamsonia plant

Some giant dinosaurs had **hollow bones** so they were not as heavy as you would think!

Parasaurolophus

para-saw-roh-LOAF-uss
Near-crested lizard

Parasaurolophus' head crest was actually a **long nasal passage** that acted as a megaphone for making **really loud noises**! It's not certain what Parasaurolophus sounded like, but it's probable their calls could travel **great distances**.

Parasaurolophus' skin was covered in small, rounded scales.

A Parasaurolophus head crest grew up to 1 m (3 ft 3 in) long!

Scientists study **birds, lizards, and crocodiles** to see how dinosaurs would have **behaved.**

Pelecanimimus

pela-kan-i-MIME-mus

Pelican mimic

A small dinosaur that was **covered in feathers**, Pelecanimimus was unusual because **it had teeth** – most bird-mimics had only beaks. This dinosaur waded into shallow waters and **waited for fish** to swim by, much like cranes do today.

The long neck of Pelecanimimus would have allowed it to reach deep into the water to catch food.

Modern birds evolved from small theropods, but these ancient relatives didn't have beaks — they had **snouts**!

Ginkgo tree

Phorusrhacos

for-us-RAH-kos
Wrinkle bearer

Phorusrhacos was a **big, flightless bird** that could probably run faster than a horse. These **fierce, meat-eating predators** are also known as "terror birds". They used their **giant spiked beaks** to capture small prey and scare away competitors. These birds belong to a subgroup of dinosaurs.

The Pleuromeia plant had no branches.

The sharp and pointed tip of Phorusrhacos' beak was a useful tool. It was probably used to hunt smaller animals and to pick away at any food it could find.

Incredibly long legs helped this meat-eater chase down even the speediest prey.

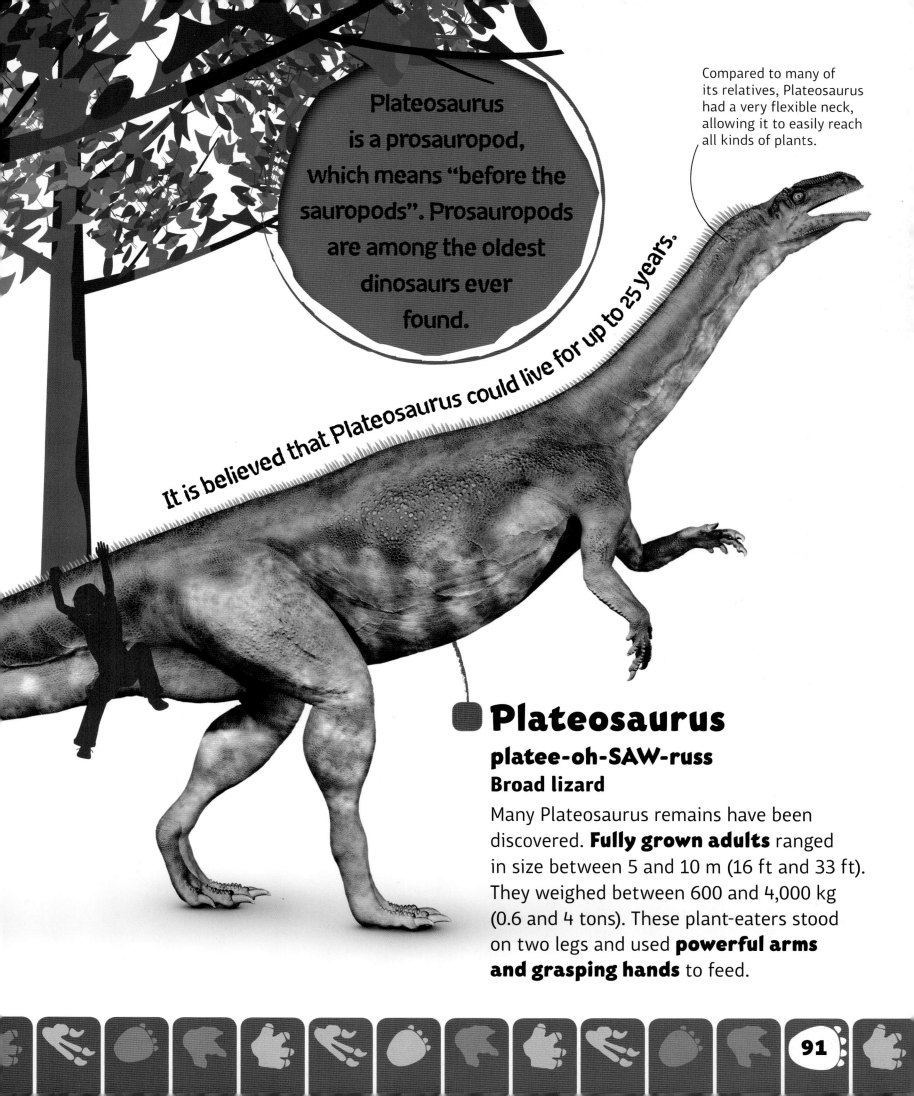

Plateosaurus is a prosauropod, which means "before the sauropods". Prosauropods are among the oldest dinosaurs ever found.

Compared to many of its relatives, Plateosaurus had a very flexible neck, allowing it to easily reach all kinds of plants.

It is believed that Plateosaurus could live for up to 25 years.

Plateosaurus
platee-oh-SAW-russ
Broad lizard

Many Plateosaurus remains have been discovered. **Fully grown adults** ranged in size between 5 and 10 m (16 ft and 33 ft). They weighed between 600 and 4,000 kg (0.6 and 4 tons). These plant-eaters stood on two legs and used **powerful arms and grasping hands** to feed.

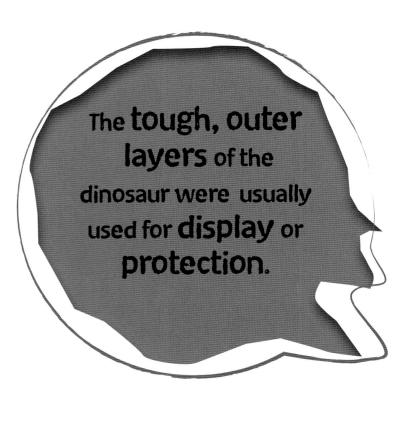

The **tough, outer layers** of the dinosaur were usually used for **display** or **protection**.

Prestosuchus

presto-sou-cus
Presto's crocodile

Prestosuchus might look like a dinosaur, but it's actually more closely related to today's **crocodiles**. Its femur (leg bone) was pressed up against its pelvis (hip bone). This meant that the **shape of its hips** differed greatly from that of a dinosaur's, which had a ball and socket joint.

NOT A DINOSAUR

Prenocephale

PREN-a-sef-ally
Sloped head

Only **a skull** of Prenocephale has been discovered. Prenocephale belonged to the group of dinosaurs called pachycephalosaur. But even with a head and teeth to study, paleontologists (dinosaur experts) still aren't sure what this **80-million-year-old** dinosaur ate.

Prestosuchus grew to more than 5 m (16 ft) in length and had lots of jagged teeth.

The Araucaria, or monkey puzzle tree, has stiff, spiky leaves.

There were **many types** of animals alive in the Mesozoic Era, including sharks, frogs, mammals, and insects.

Psittacosaurus

si-tak-ah-SAW-russ
Parrot lizard

One of the earliest and smallest of all ceratopsians, Psittacosaurus had a sharp beak, **a body covered in scales**, and hollow bristles that were 16 cm (6 in) long attached to the length of its tail. It is one of the best known dinosaurs, as **hundreds of its skeletons** have been discovered.

Protoceratops

PRO-toe-seh-rah-tops
First horned face

Protoceratops lived about 73 million years ago in China and Mongolia. It had a very large head for its body size and a **neck frill** that made it look even bigger. One amazing fossil shows it locked in a **fight with a Velociraptor**!

The head and frill of Protoceratops changed as it grew.

Psittacosaurus had a single spike-like horn sticking out from each side of its face.

Pteranodon had the perfect wing shape for gliding through the air over long distances.

Pteranodon's bones were hollow and very thin. This meant they were light and made flying easier.

Pteranodon
te-RAN-oh-don
Toothless wing

In the late Cretaceous period, Pteranodon flew through **North American skies**. It belonged to a large group of flying reptiles called **pterosaurs**. Pteranodon's **wingspan** could reach more than 6 m (20 ft) – that's about half the length of a bus!

Pterosaurs had skin covered in a type of fur, called pycnofibres.

Flying reptiles, such as Pteranodon and Pterodactylus, are often mistaken for dinosaurs. In fact, they belong to a different group of animals known as **pterosaurs**.

NOT A DINOSAUR

Pterodactylus

terra-DACT-aluss

Winged flyer

Probably the **most famous** of all the pterosaurs, Pterodactylus had a head crest and a wingspan of up to 1 m (3 ft 3 in). It hunted by **swooping down** to snatch fish and small land animals using its **sharp, cone-shaped teeth**.

NOT A DINOSAUR

Pterosaurs were the first group of vertebrates to develop powered flight.

Dinosaur diets

During the Mesozoic Era, dinosaurs lived all over Earth because they had learned to find, hunt, and eat all sorts of foods. Scientists can work out what foods dinosaurs ate based on where they were found, their teeth, and even their fossilized stomach contents!

Allosaurus

Walnut trees grew at the time of the dinosaurs.

Many types of ginkgo tree grew all over the world alongside the dinosaurs.

Herbivores

There were more plant-eaters (herbivores) than other kinds of dinosaurs. Leaves, grasses, mosses, and seeds gave them the energy to escape predators.

Apatosaurus

Stegosaurus

Hazelnut trees were common in dinosaur times.

Dinosaurs ate prehistoric dragonflies but these insects were omnivores, too.

Carnivores

Some meat-eating dinosaurs were no bigger than a cat, while others grew to be bigger than a bus. Many prehistoric animal fossils show evidence of tooth scars from hungry meat-eaters of all sizes.

Meat-eating dinosaurs fed on other dinosaurs. Some also ate mammals, fish, and reptiles.

Tyrannosaurus rex

Omnivores

Omnivores eat plants and meat. These adventurous eaters were able to find and eat plants, nuts, insects, animals, and even other dinosaurs. There were fewer omnivores than herbivores or carnivores.

Oviraptor

Gallimimus

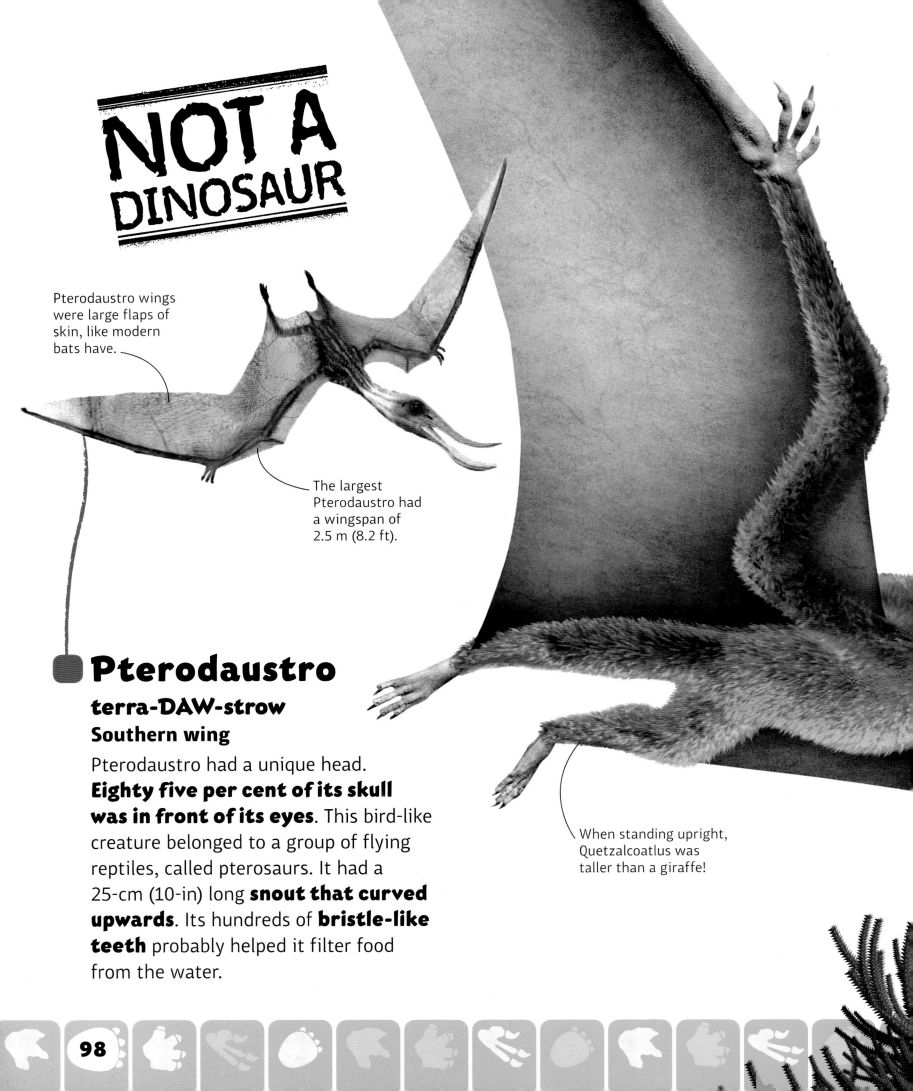

NOT A DINOSAUR

Pterodaustro wings were large flaps of skin, like modern bats have.

The largest Pterodaustro had a wingspan of 2.5 m (8.2 ft).

Pterodaustro

terra-DAW-strow
Southern wing

Pterodaustro had a unique head. **Eighty five per cent of its skull was in front of its eyes**. This bird-like creature belonged to a group of flying reptiles, called pterosaurs. It had a 25-cm (10-in) long **snout that curved upwards**. Its hundreds of **bristle-like teeth** probably helped it filter food from the water.

When standing upright, Quetzalcoatlus was taller than a giraffe!

Many flying reptiles had **large throats** to help them **swallow larger prey**.

NOT A DINOSAUR

Quetzalcoatlus

ket-zal-KWAT-luss
Named after Aztec god, Quetzalcoatl

Quetzalcoatlus is the **largest animal to ever take flight**. It had a wingspan of 12 m (39 ft 4 in). Its bones were light and hollow. This meant it could **fly, glide, and soar** for great distances.

Quetzalcoatlus didn't have teeth and probably swallowed its prey whole.

Paleontologists think Quetzalcoatlus weighed around 200 kg (440 lb). That's about the same as a dolphin.

Araucaria, or monkey puzzle tree

Sauroposeidon was a massive long-necked dinosaur that lived 110 million years ago in central North America.

Saltasaurus

SALL-ta-SAW-russ
Lizard from Salta

When dinosaur experts discovered Saltasaurus in **South America**, they thought it was a type of ankylosaur. That's because it had **bony plates** that acted as **body armour**. It is one of only a few long-neck dinosaurs ever found with bony plates stuck into its skin. These plates are called osteoderms.

Saltasaurus used its back legs to dig holes for its eggs.

At about 10 m (33 ft) in length, Saltasaurus was one of the smallest sauropods.

A sauropod's **legs** were directly under its body, like columns, because they **supported its weight.**

Ferns looked like today's species.

Saurolophus

saw-roh-LOAF-uss

Lizard crest

Saurolophus had a **crest** on top of its head. The crest pointed back away from its eyes at a 45-degree angle and it **grew larger** as Saurolophus got older. This plant-eater could walk on **two or four legs** as it searched for food. We know a lot about this dinosaur because lots of fossils have been found in North America and Asia.

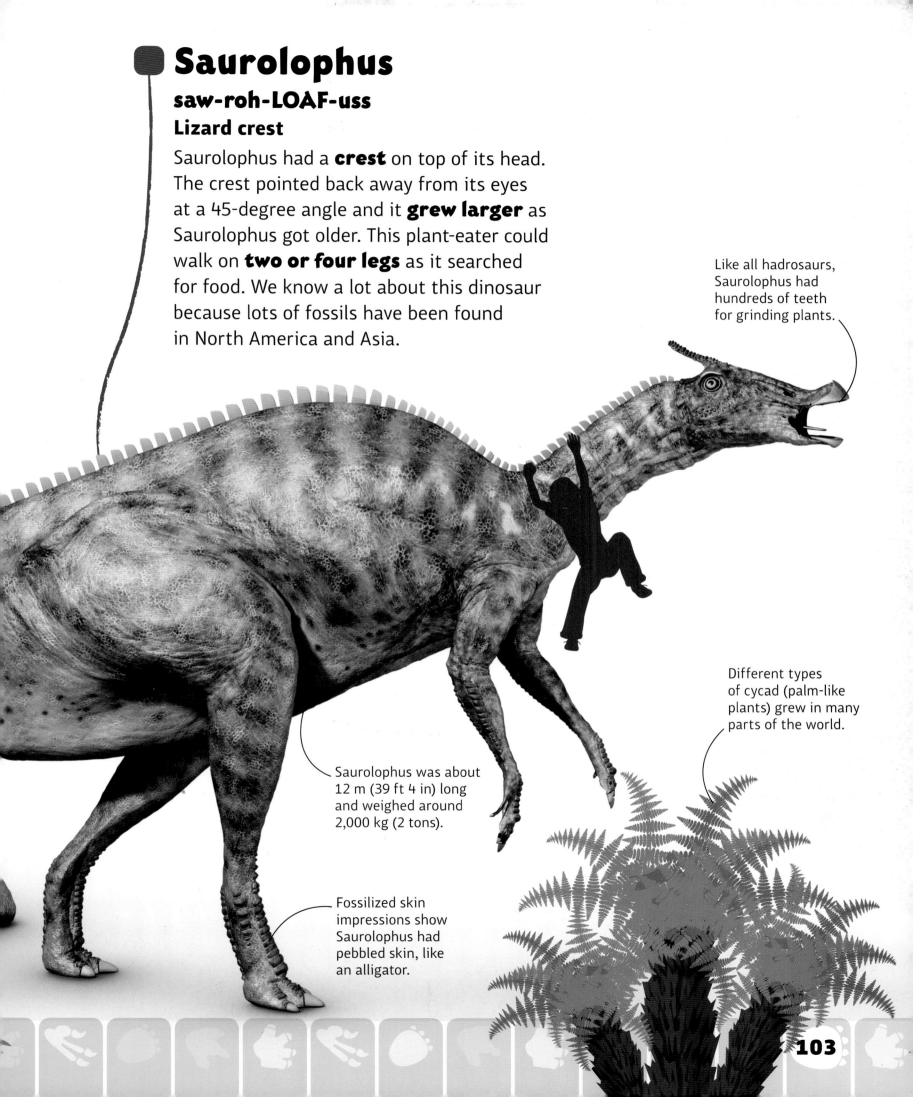

Like all hadrosaurs, Saurolophus had hundreds of teeth for grinding plants.

Different types of cycad (palm-like plants) grew in many parts of the world.

Saurolophus was about 12 m (39 ft 4 in) long and weighed around 2,000 kg (2 tons).

Fossilized skin impressions show Saurolophus had pebbled skin, like an alligator.

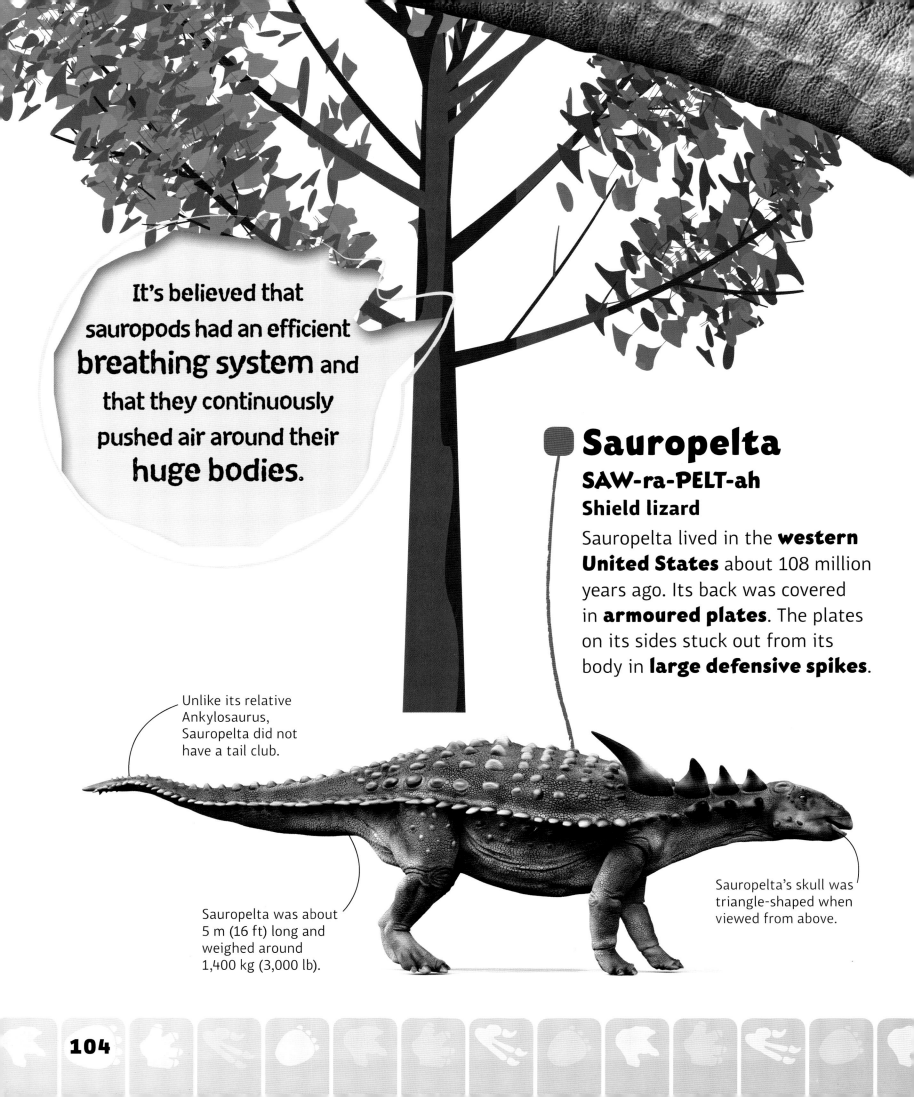

It's believed that sauropods had an efficient **breathing system** and that they continuously pushed air around their **huge bodies.**

Sauropelta
SAW-ra-PELT-ah
Shield lizard

Sauropelta lived in the **western United States** about 108 million years ago. Its back was covered in **armoured plates**. The plates on its sides stuck out from its body in **large defensive spikes**.

Unlike its relative Ankylosaurus, Sauropelta did not have a tail club.

Sauropelta was about 5 m (16 ft) long and weighed around 1,400 kg (3,000 lb).

Sauropelta's skull was triangle-shaped when viewed from above.

Ginkgo tree

Relative to its body size, **Sauroposeidon** had one of the **smallest heads** of any animal!

Sauroposeidon

saw-ra-pos-i-den
Earthquake god lizard

Dinosaur experts believe Sauroposeidon's head could have reached **18 m (59 ft) high**. This meant it could have **eaten from treetops** that not even a Diplodocus could reach. This towering "earthquake god lizard" certainly lives up to its name!

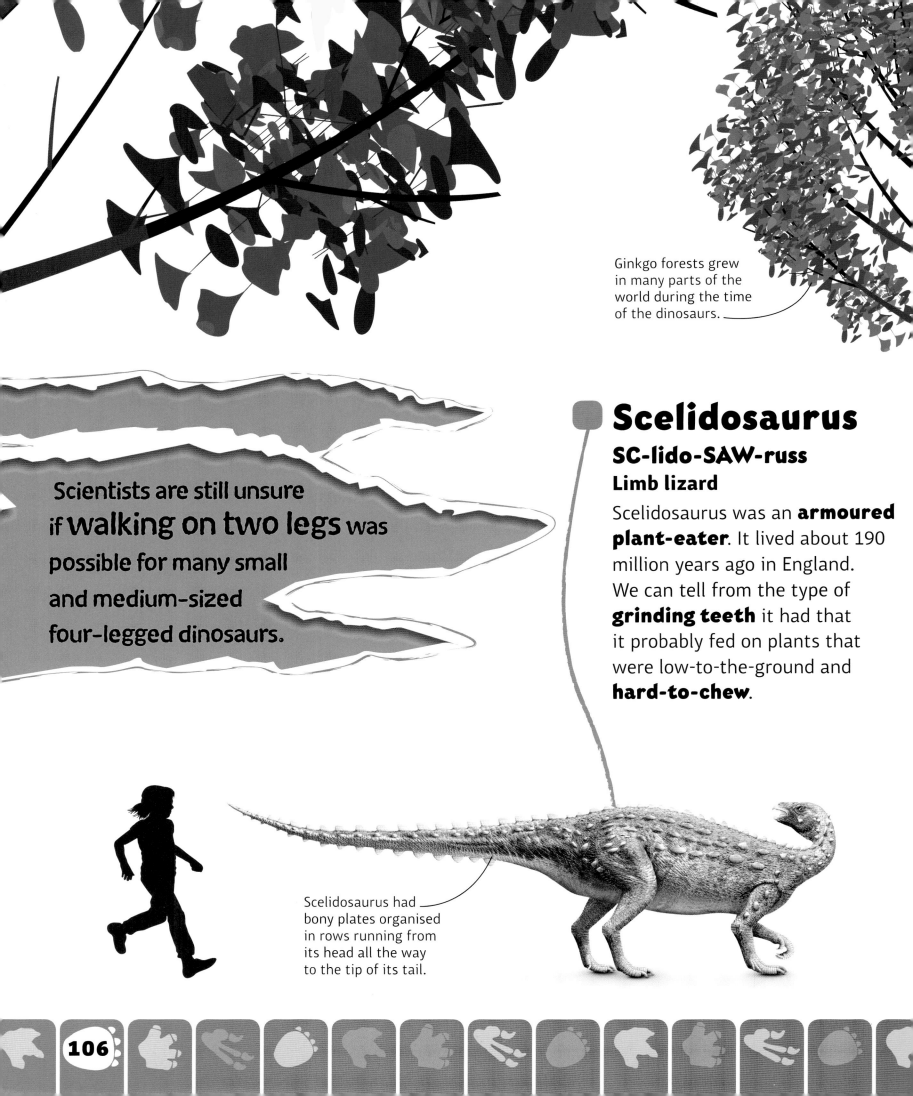

Ginkgo forests grew in many parts of the world during the time of the dinosaurs.

Scientists are still unsure if **walking on two legs** was possible for many small and medium-sized four-legged dinosaurs.

Scelidosaurus
SC-lido-SAW-russ
Limb lizard

Scelidosaurus was an **armoured plant-eater**. It lived about 190 million years ago in England. We can tell from the type of **grinding teeth** it had that it probably fed on plants that were low-to-the-ground and **hard-to-chew**.

Scelidosaurus had bony plates organised in rows running from its head all the way to the tip of its tail.

Many species of dinosaurs had **long feathers** on their arms and legs, even though they couldn't fly.

Scutellosaurus

sc–tella-SAW-russ
Little-shielded lizard

Weighing in at only 10 kg (22 lb), Scutellosaurus was a **very small** plant-eater. For added protection, this dinosaur had **two rows of bony plates** running the length of its back. Scientists believe it often **stood up** on two legs to make itself appear larger or to reach food.

Sinornithosaurus

si-NOR-nith-oh-SAW-russ
Chinese bird-lizard

Sinornithosaurus was a small, feathered theropod that **lived in China** 123 million years ago. Skeletons have revealed that this dinosaur was **covered in feathers**. It may have used these to glide from tree to tree or to **swoop down on prey**.

Sinornithosaurus only weighed about 3 kg (6 lb 10 oz). That's about the size of a small fox.

The long tail of Spinosaurus may have helped it to swim through water as it hunted.

Spinosaurus looked like a two-humped camel. It had a unique sail along its back with a dip in the middle.

Sinosauropteryx

SINE-oh-SAW-op-ter-ICKS

Chinese reptilian wing

Sinosauropteryx was a close relative of Compsognathus and one of the first non-flying dinosaurs to be found with **evidence of feathers**. Its remains were so well-preserved that scientists could even work out its **main colour** – different shades of brown.

A Sinosauropteryx was around 1 m (3 ft 3 in) in length – half of which was its tail.

Tempskya

Like today's crocodiles, Spinosaurus may have used the tiny holes along its skull to sense where fish were hiding when it was hunting head-first in water.

At about 15 m (49 ft) long, Spinosaurus may have been the **largest meat-eater** ever to have walked the Earth.

Spinosaurus

SPINE-oh-SAW-russ

Spine lizard

Spinosaurus had a sail on its back and **long, narrow jaws** that were perfect for hunting in water. It may have been one of the only large carnivorous dinosaurs that spent large amounts of time **in the water**.

Eggs and nests

Like all reptiles, baby dinosaurs hatched from eggs laid by their mothers. Just like birds today, many dinosaur species sat on nests to warm and protect their eggs. Once they hatched, some young dinosaurs were looked after by parents, while others were left to fend for themselves.

Inside an egg

Experts think that some baby dinosaurs stayed inside eggs for many weeks before hatching. The amount of time probably varied greatly from one species to another.

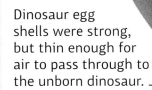

The shape of this unborn dinosaur inside its egg gives us clues to how dinosaurs' bodies changed and grew over time.

Dinosaur egg shells were strong, but thin enough for air to pass through to the unborn dinosaur.

Protoceratops laid lots of eggs in a single nest.

Dinosaur nests

Just like modern birds, dinosaurs made their nests from twigs, mud, and leaves. Experts found fossilized remains of more than ten young Protoceratops in a nest. They think young dinosaurs may have lived in groups.

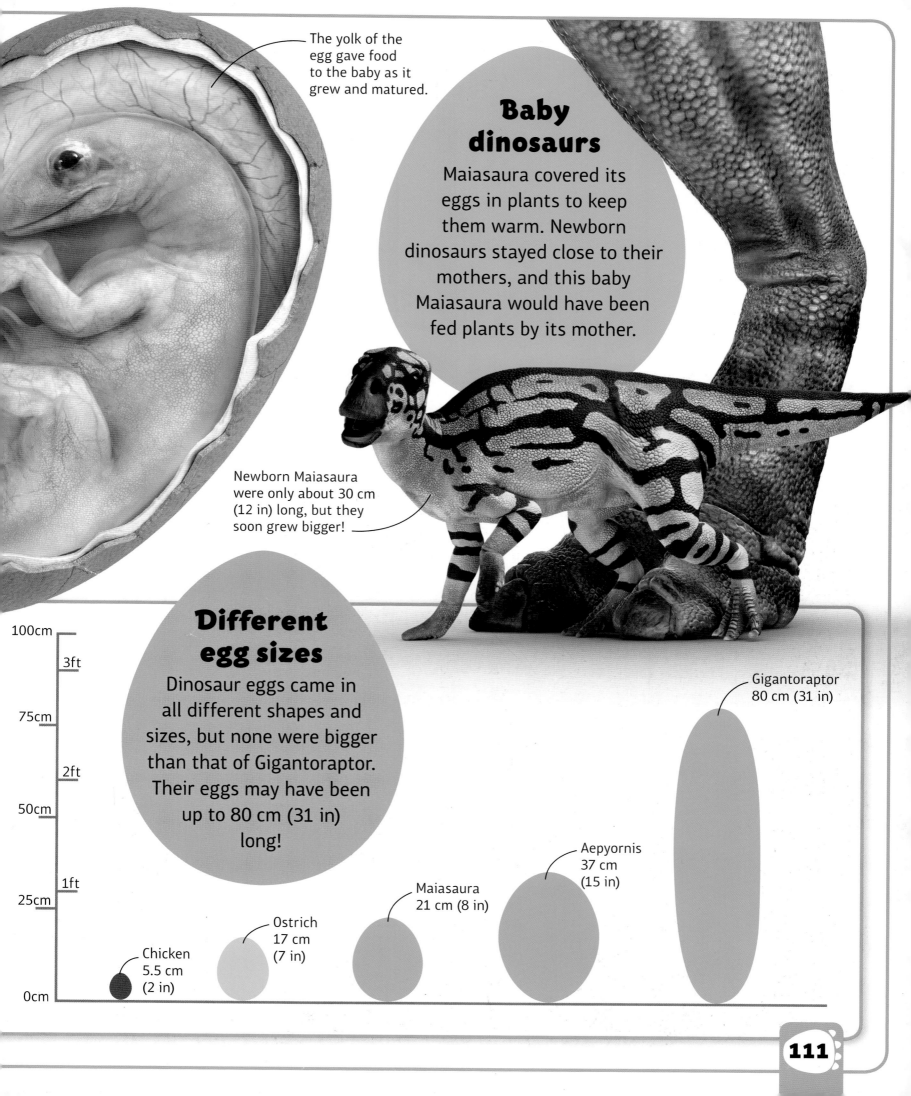

The yolk of the egg gave food to the baby as it grew and matured.

Baby dinosaurs

Maiasaura covered its eggs in plants to keep them warm. Newborn dinosaurs stayed close to their mothers, and this baby Maiasaura would have been fed plants by its mother.

Newborn Maiasaura were only about 30 cm (12 in) long, but they soon grew bigger!

Different egg sizes

Dinosaur eggs came in all different shapes and sizes, but none were bigger than that of Gigantoraptor. Their eggs may have been up to 80 cm (31 in) long!

Gigantoraptor
80 cm (31 in)

Aepyornis
37 cm
(15 in)

Maiasaura
21 cm (8 in)

Ostrich
17 cm
(7 in)

Chicken
5.5 cm
(2 in)

100cm
3ft
75cm
2ft
50cm
1ft
25cm
0cm

Araucaria or monkey puzzle tree

Williamsonia

A Stegosaurus' **brain** was small for its body. It was about the same size as a **dog's!**

Stegosaurus' spiky tail arrangement is called a thagomizer.

Stegoceras
STEG-oh-SEH-russ
Horned roof

This small, omnivorous dinosaur had a **thick, bony dome** on top of its head, just like a "horned roof". Paleontologists are still unsure why its head looked like this.

Stegoceras was much smaller than its close relative, Pachycephalosaurus. It was about the size of a goat.

Stegosaurus

STEG-oh-SAW-russ
Roofed lizard

Stegosaurus was a **slow mover** with a tiny brain, but it had other plus points. It probably used its 1-m (3-ft 3-in) **tail spikes** to defend itself. Its **plates** may have helped Stegosaurus seem bigger to dinosaurs who were looking for a fight.

Stegosaurus plates were criss-crossed with **blood vessels**, which may have helped it keep a comfortable body temperature.

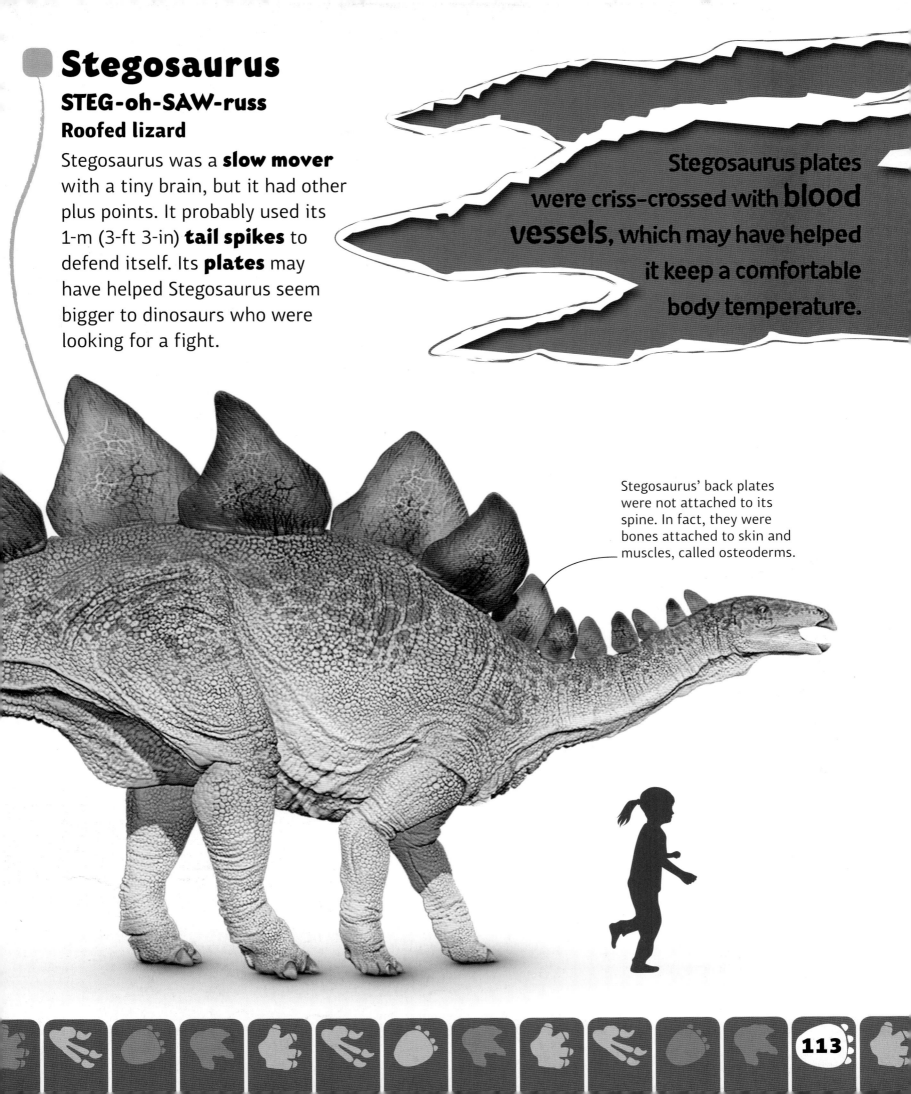

Stegosaurus' back plates were not attached to its spine. In fact, they were bones attached to skin and muscles, called osteoderms.

Ornithomimids, such as Struthiomimus, were the **fastest group** of dinosaurs on Earth.

Struthiomimus

STREW-theo-MY-muss
Ostrich mimic

Struthiomimus lived in North America about 70 million years ago. Gorgosaurus and Daspletosaurus hunted this **feathered dinosaur**. Struthiomimus could run at speeds of up to 80 kph (50 mph).

Struthiomimus had a stiff and rigid tail, used for balance while running.

Giant sequoia trees are still around today.

Styracosaurus' **six spikes** were probably used to **spot other Styracosauruses** and to attract a mate.

Styracosaurus

sty-RACK-oh-SAW-russ
Spiked lizard

Styracosaurus lived a few million years before its close relative, Triceratops. It had a **horn on each cheek**, a longer, single nose horn, and up to **six long spikes** sticking out from the top of the frill that covered its neck. Smaller spikes ran from its frill to the end of its tail.

Styracosaurus' nose horn was about 50 cm (20 in) long.

Supersaurus remains have been discovered in both North America and Europe.

Suchomimus' teeth were long, cone-shaped spikes.

Suchomimus may have had webbed feet to help it walk about in its swampy home.

Suchomimus

SOO-ka-MIME-uss
Crocodile mimic

Egypt used to be swampland, making it the **perfect hunting ground** for Suchomimus. This relative of Spinosaurus was very good at **hunting large fish** and marine reptiles. It had **long, narrow jaws**, like a crocodile, with more than 120 teeth.

Scientists think
Supersaurus was
one of the largest
animals to walk the
Earth in the Jurassic
period, 153 million
years ago.

Some experts
think that both
Supersaurus and
Suchomimus had
small **pointy spines**
that ran all the way
down their backs!

100 million years ago, western North America was a **lush landscape** filled with plants such as ginkgos, ferns, and cycads.

Ginkgo plant

There is good evidence to suggest that Tenontosaurus was hunted by Deinonychus.

Supersaurus

super-SAW-russ
Super lizard

Supersaurus was also once called **Ultrasauros**. It had one of the **longest known sauropod necks** compared to its body length. It weighed about 40,000 kg (44 tons). That's as heavy as **two trucks loaded with concrete**.

Ferns

Tenontosaurus

t-non-ta-SAW-russ

Sinew lizard

Tenontosaurus was a **medium-sized ornithopod**. It grew up to 8 m (26 ft) long and weighed almost 2,000 kg (2 tons). Examples of this plant-eating dinosaur have almost been **frozen in time**. Scientists could tell that some females were expecting a baby when they died.

A Supersaurus skull has not yet been found. Scientists use the skulls of close relatives to guess what its head looked like.

Tenontosaurus had a U-shaped beak used to bite through plants.

Cycad plant

Therizinosaurus was 10 m
(33 ft) long and weighed
about 5,000 kg (5 tons).
It was the largest member
of the maniraptoran group.

Araucaria, or
monkey-puzzle
tree

Therizinosaurus

thera-ZINA-SAW-russ
Scythe lizard

Therizinosaurus is one of the
strangest-looking dinosaurs. Not
only was this plant-eater **covered
in feathers**, but it also had the
largest claws ever known.
They grew up to 1 m (3 ft 3 in) long.

They may look like
deadly hunting tools,
but experts believe
Therizinosaurus used
these huge claws for
ripping up plants.

Ferns grew
everywhere.

Torosaurus and Triceratops were **very similar**. Some experts even think they may have been one species whose **shape changed** as it grew.

Scientists use the size and shape of frills to identify similar dinosaurs like Torosaurus, Albertaceratops, and Styracosaurus.

Torosaurus fossils were first found in 1891, in the western United States.

Torosaurus
TOH-row-SAW-russ
Perforated lizard

Torosaurus had one of the **largest skulls** of any known land animal. Its skull was almost 3 m (10 ft) long. Much like Triceratops, Torosaurus had **two large horns** just above its eyes, but its nose horns were much smaller than its relative's.

Triceratops

try-serra-tops
Three horned face

Triceratops is by far the most famous of all the **horned dinosaurs**. It had **three horns**, a beak like a parrot's, and an enormous frill. T. rex liked to eat Triceratops and experts think they probably travelled in herds for protection against these top hunters.

Experts think a **giant meteor** hit the Earth 65.5 million years ago, killing many animals and plants, including all the dinosaurs, making them **extinct.**

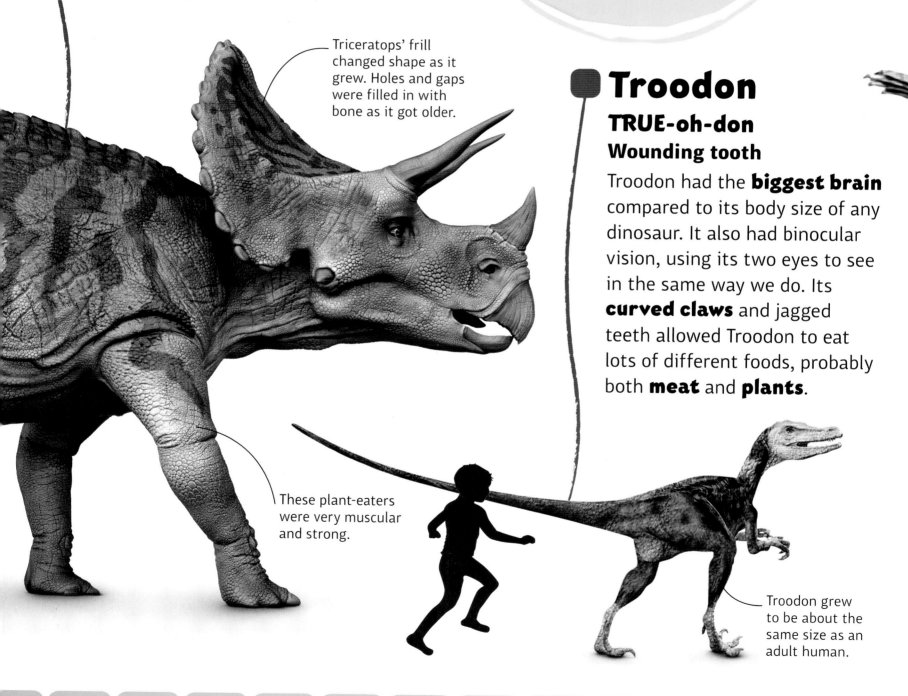

Triceratops' frill changed shape as it grew. Holes and gaps were filled in with bone as it got older.

These plant-eaters were very muscular and strong.

Troodon

TRUE-oh-don
Wounding tooth

Troodon had the **biggest brain** compared to its body size of any dinosaur. It also had binocular vision, using its two eyes to see in the same way we do. Its **curved claws** and jagged teeth allowed Troodon to eat lots of different foods, probably both **meat** and **plants**.

Troodon grew to be about the same size as an adult human.

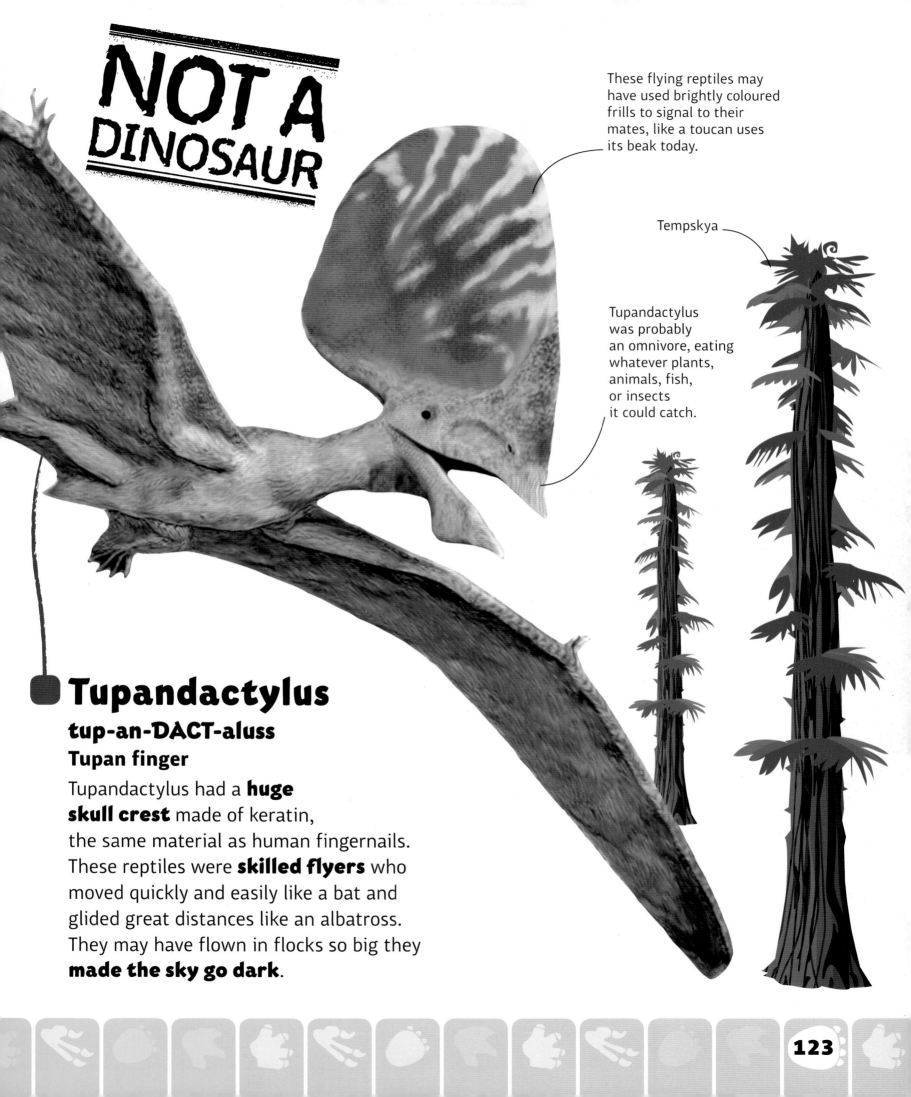

NOT A DINOSAUR

These flying reptiles may have used brightly coloured frills to signal to their mates, like a toucan uses its beak today.

Tempskya

Tupandactylus was probably an omnivore, eating whatever plants, animals, fish, or insects it could catch.

Tupandactylus

tup-an-DACT-aluss

Tupan finger

Tupandactylus had a **huge skull crest** made of keratin, the same material as human fingernails. These reptiles were **skilled flyers** who moved quickly and easily like a bat and glided great distances like an albatross. They may have flown in flocks so big they **made the sky go dark**.

Small dinosaurs

Dinosaurs came in all different shapes and sizes, and even though the largest ones are probably the most famous, small dinosaurs were amazing, too. Specialized survival features meant some of these dinosaurs were so successful that they're still alive today – we call them birds!

Anchiornis is one of the **smallest dinosaurs** ever found. It was about 40 cm (16 in) long.

Chicken

Scientists put animals into special groups according to features that they share. Just like humans are a special type of ape, birds are a special type of dinosaur... and the only ones still alive today!

Sinornithosaurus

Paleontologists have been able to work out the colour of Sinornithosaurus' feathers. They were very colourful – a mix of yellow, reddish-brown, grey, and black! Some experts once even suggested they had a venomous bite.

Dilong

Dilong was a meat-eating dinosaur that lived about 125 million years ago in China. This theropod walked on two legs, which were covered in scales. The rest of its body had lots of soft feathers to keep it warm.

Microraptor

Microraptor was a small, four-winged theropod that lived 120 million years ago in China. It may have used its wings to capture prey and then press down on the animal so it couldn't escape.

Ferns

Stegoceras

Stegoceras lived in western Canada. It had a dome-shaped head like its relative, Pachycephalosaurus, but it was much smaller. Stegoceras had a very thick skull. Experts think it may have helped it in the fight for mates.

Velociraptor

Velociraptor was first discovered in 1923 in Mongolia. We now know it was covered in feathers. True to its name of "speedy thief", Velociraptor used its tail for balance as it ran at great speed! It may have hunted in packs and often preyed upon Protoceratops.

Ginkgo plant

Many of Tyrannosaurus' **relatives had feathers**, including the smaller and faster Dilong.

Tyrannosaurus rex had binocular vision, like humans have. This helped it to find and hunt prey.

Experts think T. rex could munch up to 230 kg (500 lb) in one bite. That's the same as being able to put a whole grizzly bear in your mouth at once!

Even though almost all of its theropod relatives had three fingers, T. rex only had two.

Tyrannosaurus rex

tie-RAN-oh-SAW-russ reks
King of the tyrant lizards

Called T. rex for short, these huge meat-eaters had an **incredibly strong bite** and big teeth that grew to be 30 cm (12 in) long. Each tooth had two sharp, jagged edges, like a double-sided knife. To make them even more deadly, they could run as fast as 29 kph (18 mph).

Velociraptors weighed about **15 kg** (33 lb), which is the same as a medium-sized dog.

Utahraptor

U-ta-RAP-tor

Utah's seizer

Utahraptor lived about 126 million years ago in western North America. It is the biggest **feathered dinosaur** in the Dromaeosauridae family. Utahraptor was a swift runner that weighed almost 500 kg (0.5 tons). It may have **hunted in packs** to bring down large prey.

Utahraptor had large, slashing claws on its inner toes. These may have helped it grip the ground as it ran.

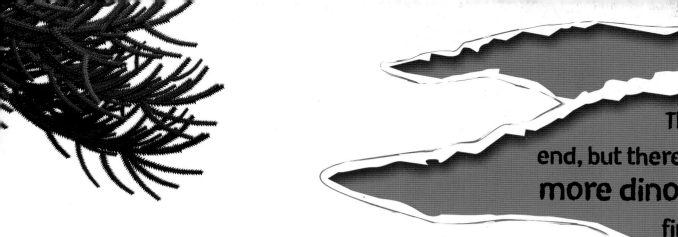

This parade is at an end, but there are **hundreds more dinosaurs** for you to find out about… or even **discover!**

Velociraptor

ve-LOSS-ee-RAP-tor
Swift seizer

Velociraptor had **feathers** that were probably used for display, as well as **warmth**. They also had **curved claws**. This dinosaur could not fly, but like an eagle, it used its curved claws to pin its prey in place.

Zuniceratops

zoo-nee-ser-ah-tops
Zuni-horned face

Zuniceratops lived **10 million years** before most of its **horned and crested relatives**. By comparing its remains with the remains of later dinosaurs such as Triceratops, Styracosaurus, and Centrosaurus, we can learn lots about how these amazing animals **changed to survive**, and thrive, in the dangerous world around them.

At only 150 kg (330 lb), Zuniceratops was much smaller than its close relative, Triceratops.

End of the dinosaurs

About 66 million years ago a meteorite the size of Mount Everest crashed into the Earth near what is now Mexico. The impact caused tidal waves, global wildfires, and altered the climate for thousands of years. It marked the end of 75 per cent of all life on Earth, including all non-flying dinosaurs.

Meteorite strikes

The meteorite impact would have greatly heated the planet by throwing huge amounts of hot dirt and ash into the atmosphere.

Darkness descends

Soot from the impact of the meteorite was thrown into the sky and blocked out the Sun for years.

Earth cools

Less sunlight resulted in less heat. As the planet cooled, many plants and animals struggled to survive.

Who survived?

Even though the meteorite impact led to the extinction of the dinosaurs, many other types of animal were able to survive and flourish.

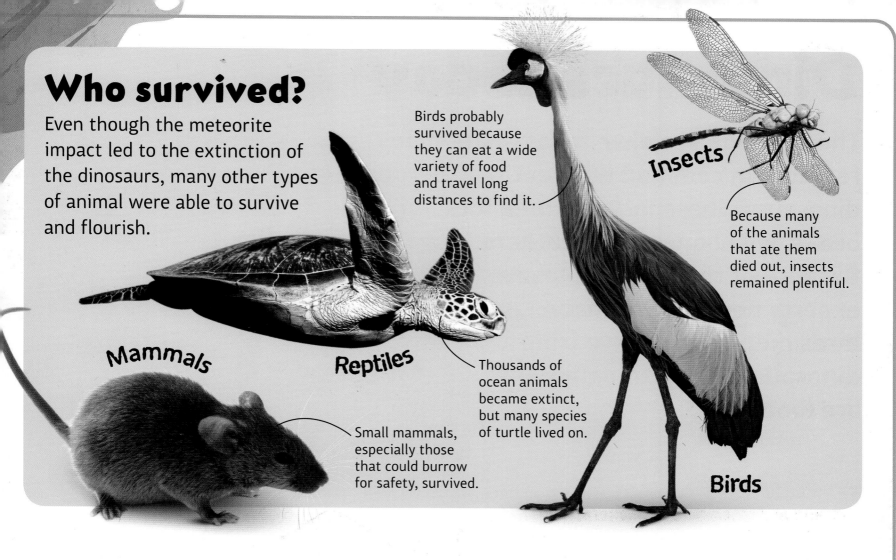

Birds probably survived because they can eat a wide variety of food and travel long distances to find it.

Insects

Because many of the animals that ate them died out, insects remained plentiful.

Mammals

Reptiles

Thousands of ocean animals became extinct, but many species of turtle lived on.

Small mammals, especially those that could burrow for safety, survived.

Birds

Herbivores die

With far fewer plants to eat, many plant-eating dinosaurs, especially the largest that needed a lot of food, began to die off.

Carnivores die

Finally, with fewer and fewer herbivores to hunt, meat-eating dinosaurs saw their food sources disappear. They, too, became extinct.

Dinosaurs today

The birds we see alive today share many features in common with extinct theropod dinosaurs. These include three toes, beaks, wishbones, and feathers. Because of this, most dinosaur experts now believe that birds didn't just evolve from dinosaurs – they actually are dinosaurs.

The shape and size of modern bird brains help us to better understand the brains of their extinct dinosaur relatives.

Feathers help birds and dinosaurs stay warm, signal to mates, and sometimes glide and fly.

Theropods, including all living birds, are a group of animals that walk upright on two legs.

The term "theropod" means "beast-footed".

Birds

Birds today come in all different shapes and sizes, just like dinosaurs did. Their wing and beak shapes vary a lot, but all are adapted to help the bird survive in its environment, just like dinosaurs.

Chickens rarely use their wings for flight.

Even small birds, like this Eurasian songbird, are descended from dinosaurs.

A chicken's large crest is used to attract mates, just like a dinosaur crest is.

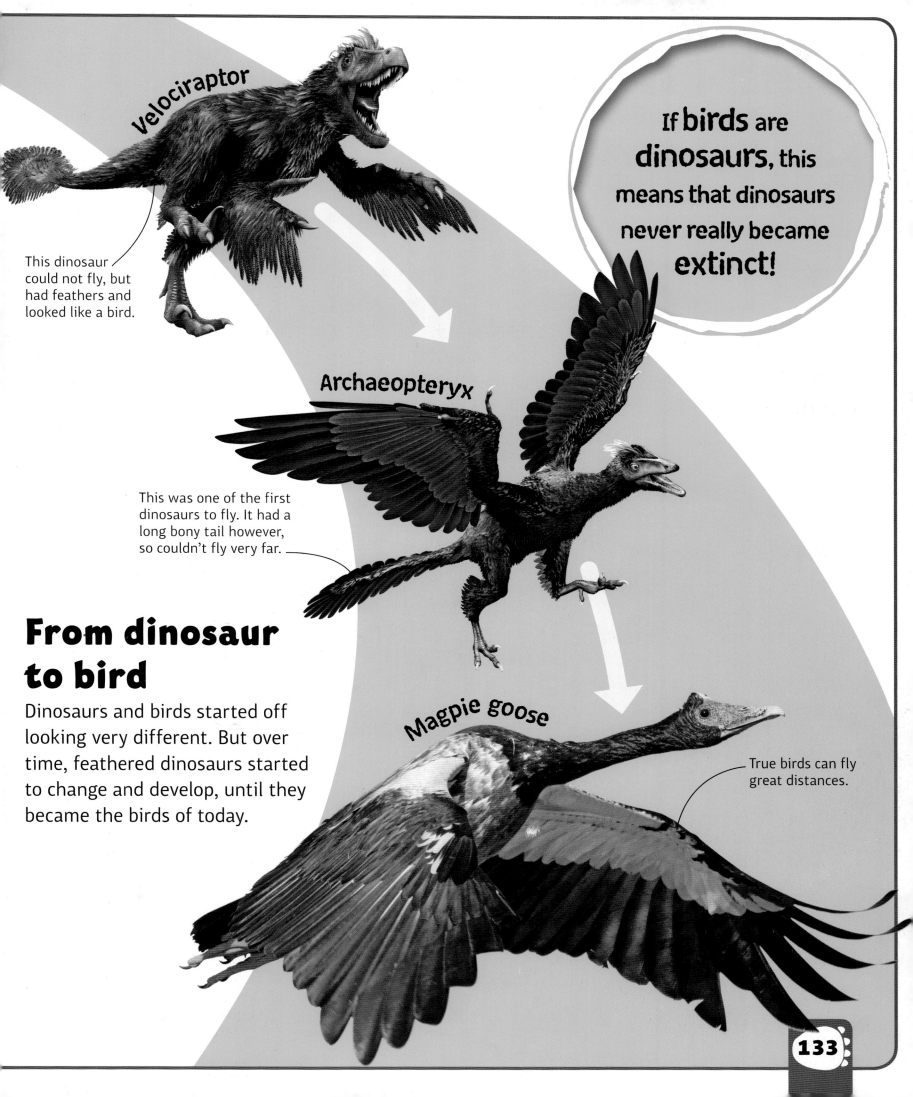

Velociraptor

This dinosaur could not fly, but had feathers and looked like a bird.

If **birds** are **dinosaurs**, this means that dinosaurs never really became **extinct!**

Archaeopteryx

This was one of the first dinosaurs to fly. It had a long bony tail however, so couldn't fly very far.

From dinosaur to bird

Dinosaurs and birds started off looking very different. But over time, feathered dinosaurs started to change and develop, until they became the birds of today.

Magpie goose

True birds can fly great distances.

Dino file

Here are key facts and figures about all the dinosaurs that parade through this book.

Key

- Group
- Where found
- Length
- Weight
- Permian
- Triassic
- Jurrasic
- Cretaceous
- Miocene

Argentinosaurus
- Sauropod / Argentina
- 39 m (128 ft)
- 82,000 kg (180,000 lb)

Abelisaurus
- Theropod / Argentina
- 9 m (30 ft)
- 900 kg (2,000 lb)

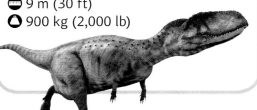

Amargasaurus
- Sauropod / Argentina
- 10 m (33 ft) / 2,720 kg (6,000 lb)

Austroraptor
- Theropod / Argentina
- 5 m (16 ft)
- 365 kg (810 lb)

Albertaceratops
- Ceratopsian / Canada
- 6 m (20 ft) / 3,500 kg (7,700 lb)

Anchiornis
- Theropod / China
- 0.5 m (20 in)
- 110 g (4 oz)

Barosaurus
- Sauropod / USA
- 26 m (85 ft)
- 18,000 kg (39,700 lb)

Ankylosaurus
- Ankylosaur / North America
- 6 m (20 ft) / 5,440 kg (12,000 lb)

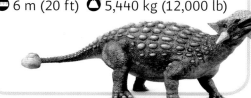

Baryonyx
- Theropod / Europe
- 7 m (23 ft) / 1,090 kg (2,400 lb)

Albertosaurus
- Theropod / Canada
- 9 m (30 ft)
- 1,360 kg (3,000 lb)

Apatosaurus
- Sauropod / USA
- 22 m (72 ft)
- 20,000 kg (44,000 lb)

Brachiosaurus
- Sauropod / USA
- 26 m (85 ft)
- 30,800 kg (68,000 lb)

Allosaurus
- Theropod / Portugal, USA
- 9 m (30 ft)
- 2,085 kg (4,600 lb)

Archaeopteryx
- Theropod / Germany
- 0.5 m (2 ft) / 1 kg (2 lb)

Brachylophosaurus
- Hadrosaur / North America
- 11 m (36 ft) / 6,350 kg (14,000 lb)

Camarasaurus
- Sauropod
- USA
- 23 m (75 ft)
- 42,600 kg (94,000 lb)

Camptosaurus
- Iguanadont
- USA
- 6 m (20 ft)
- 850 kg (1,874 lb)

Carcharodontosaurus
- Theropod
- Algeria, Niger, Tunisia
- 13 m (43 ft)
- 10,886 kg (24,000 lb)

Carnotaurus
- Theropod
- Argentina
- 9 m (30 ft)
- 1,225 kg (2,700 lb)

Caudipteryx
- Theropod
- China
- 1 m (3 ft)
- 2.5 kg (5.5 lb)

Centrosaurus
- Ceratopsian
- Canada
- 6 m (20 ft)
- 1,000 kg (2,200 lb)

Ceratosaurus
- Theropod
- North America, Portugal, Tanzania
- 6 m (20 ft)
- 980 kg (2,160 lb)

Citipati
- Theropod
- Mongolia
- 2 m (7 ft)
- 50 kg (110 lb)

Coelophysis
- Theropod
- USA
- 3 m (10 ft)
- 15 kg (33 lb)

Compsognathus
- Ornithomimosaur
- Germany, France
- 1 m (3 ft)
- 3.5 kg (8 lb)

Concavenator
- Theropod
- Spain
- 6 m (20 ft)
- 980 kg (2,160 lb)

Corythosaurus
- Hadrosaur
- North America
- 8 m (26 ft)
- 4,000 kg (8,800 lb)

Cryolophosaurus
- Theropod
- Antarctica
- 6.5 m (21 ft)
- 465 kg (1,025 lb)

Daspletosaurus
- Theropod
- Canada
- 9 m (30 ft)
- 2,720 kg (6,000 lb)

Deinocheirus
- Ornithomimosaur
- Mongolia
- 11 m (36 ft)
- 5,443 kg (12,000 lb)

Deinonychus
- Theropod
- USA
- 3.5 m (11 ft)
- 73 kg (161 lb)

Dilong
- Theropod
- China
- 2 m (7 ft)
- 10 kg (22 lb)

Dilophosaurus
- Theropod / USA
- 7 m (23 ft)
- 400 kg (880 lb)

Eryops
- Temnospondyl / USA
- 3 m (10 ft)
- 90 kg (200 lb)

Giraffatitan
- Sauropod / Tanzania
- 22 m (72 ft)
- 27,200 kg (60,000 lb)

Dimetrodon
- Synapsid / North America
- 4 m (13 ft)
- 250 kg (550 lb)

Euoplocephalus
- Ankylosaur / USA
- 6 m (20 ft) / 1,800 kg (4,000 lb)

Hadrosaurus
- Hadrosaur / USA
- 9 m (29.5 ft)
- 6,350 kg (14,000 lb)

Dimorphodon
- Pterosaur / England
- 1 m (3 ft) / 2 kg (4.5 lb)

Gallimimus
- Ornithomimosaur
- Mongolia
- 8 m (26 ft)
- 450 kg (990 lb)

Herrerasaurus
- Theropod / Argentina
- 6 m (20 ft) / 350 kg (770 lb)

Diplodocus
- Sauropod
- North America
- 25 m (82 ft)
- 13,600 kg (30,000 lb)

Heterodontosaurus
- Heterodontosaur / South Africa
- 1 m (3 ft) / 10 kg (22 lb)

Dryosaurus
- Iguanadont / USA
- 4 m (13.1 ft)
- 90 kg (200 lb)

Giganotosaurus
- Theropod / Argentina
- 13 m (43 ft)
- 11,800 kg (26,000 lb)

Hypacrosaurus
- Hadrosaur
- North America
- 9 m (29.5 ft)
- 3,600 kg (8,000 lb)

Edmontosaurus
- Hadrosaur / North America
- 12 m (39.5 ft) / 3,600 kg (8,000 lb)

Gigantoraptor
- Theropod / Mongolia
- 8 m (26 ft) / 1,800 kg (4,000 lb)

Hypsilophodon
- Ornithopod / England
- 2 m (6.5 ft) / 20 kg (44 lb)

Iguanodon
- Hadrosaur / Western Europe
- 10 m (33 ft) / 3,500 kg (7,700 lb)

Masiakasaurus
- Theropod / Madagascar
- 2 m (6.5 ft)
- 35 kg (80 lb)

Ornitholestes
- Theropod
- USA
- 2 m (6.5 ft)
- 25 kg (55 lb)

Irritator
- Theropod
- Brazil
- 7.5 m (25 ft)
- 900 kg (2,000 lb)

Microraptor
- Theropod
- China
- 2 m (6.5 ft)
- 1kg (2.2 lb)

Pachycephalosaurus
- Pachycephalosaur / USA
- 4.5 m (15 ft) / 450 kg (990 lb)

Kentrosaurus
- Stegosaurian / Tanzania
- 4.5 m (15 ft)
- 900 kg (2,000 lb)

Muttaburrasaurus
- Hadrosaur / Australia
- 8 m (26 ft)
- 2,700 kg (6,000 lb)

Pachyrhinosaurus
- Ceratopsian
- North America
- 8 m (26 ft)
- 4,000 kg (8,800 lb)

Lambeosaurus
- Hadrosaur
- North America
- 9 m (29.5 ft)
- 5,000 kg (11,000 lb)

Neovenator
- Theropod / England
- 7.5 m (25 ft) / 900 kg (2,000 lb)

Parasaurolophus
- Hadrosaur / North America
- 9.5 m (31 ft)
- 2,300 kg (5,000 lb)

Maiasaura
- Hadrosaur / USA
- 9 m (30 ft) / 2,000 kg (4,400 lb)

Nigersaurus
- Sauropod / Niger
- 9 m (30 ft)
- 3,600 kg (8,000 lb)

Pelecanimimus
- Ornithomimosaur / Spain
- 2.5 m (8 ft) / 45 kg (100 lb)

Mamenchisaurus
- Sauropod / China
- 35 m (115 ft)
- 50,000 kg (110,000 lb)

Phorusrhacos
- Theropod / Argentina
- 2.5 m (8 ft)
- 130 kg (300 lb)

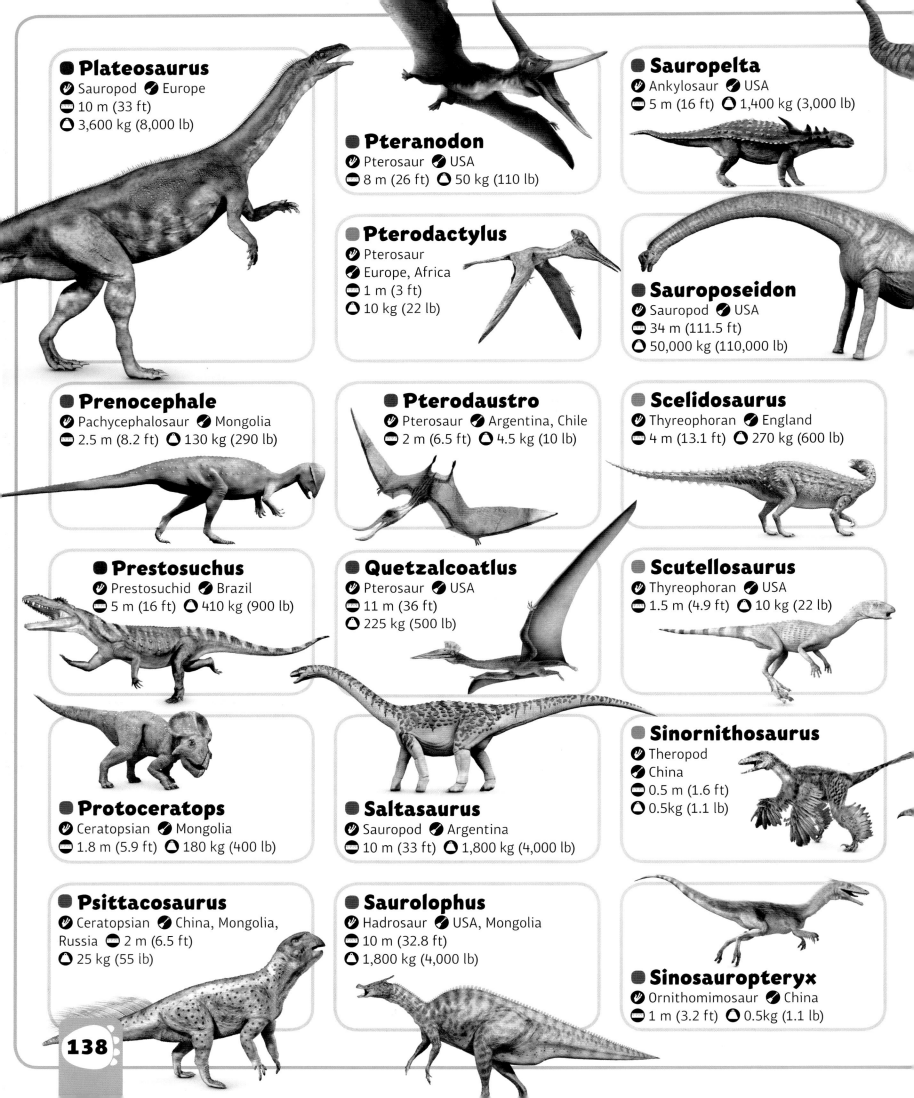

Plateosaurus
- Sauropod · Europe
- 10 m (33 ft)
- 3,600 kg (8,000 lb)

Pteranodon
- Pterosaur · USA
- 8 m (26 ft) · 50 kg (110 lb)

Pterodactylus
- Pterosaur
- Europe, Africa
- 1 m (3 ft)
- 10 kg (22 lb)

Sauropelta
- Ankylosaur · USA
- 5 m (16 ft) · 1,400 kg (3,000 lb)

Sauroposeidon
- Sauropod · USA
- 34 m (111.5 ft)
- 50,000 kg (110,000 lb)

Prenocephale
- Pachycephalosaur · Mongolia
- 2.5 m (8.2 ft) · 130 kg (290 lb)

Pterodaustro
- Pterosaur · Argentina, Chile
- 2 m (6.5 ft) · 4.5 kg (10 lb)

Scelidosaurus
- Thyreophoran · England
- 4 m (13.1 ft) · 270 kg (600 lb)

Prestosuchus
- Prestosuchid · Brazil
- 5 m (16 ft) · 410 kg (900 lb)

Quetzalcoatlus
- Pterosaur · USA
- 11 m (36 ft)
- 225 kg (500 lb)

Scutellosaurus
- Thyreophoran · USA
- 1.5 m (4.9 ft) · 10 kg (22 lb)

Protoceratops
- Ceratopsian · Mongolia
- 1.8 m (5.9 ft) · 180 kg (400 lb)

Saltasaurus
- Sauropod · Argentina
- 10 m (33 ft) · 1,800 kg (4,000 lb)

Sinornithosaurus
- Theropod
- China
- 0.5 m (1.6 ft)
- 0.5kg (1.1 lb)

Psittacosaurus
- Ceratopsian · China, Mongolia, Russia · 2 m (6.5 ft)
- 25 kg (55 lb)

Saurolophus
- Hadrosaur · USA, Mongolia
- 10 m (32.8 ft)
- 1,800 kg (4,000 lb)

Sinosauropteryx
- Ornithomimosaur · China
- 1 m (3.2 ft) · 0.5kg (1.1 lb)

Spinosaurus
- Theropod • North Africa
- 15 m (49 ft)
- 18,000 kg (40,000 lb)

Supersaurus
- Sauropod • USA
- 33 m (108 ft)
- 40,000 kg (90,000 lb)

Tupandactylus
- Pterosaur
- Brazil
- 5 m (16 ft) • 60 kg (130 lb)

Stegoceras
- Pachycephalosaur • North America
- 2 m (6.5 ft) • 35 kg (80 lb)

Tenontosaurus
- Hadrosaur • USA
- 8 m (26.2 ft) • 1,350 kg (3,000 lb)

Tyrannosaurus
- Theropod • USA
- 12 m (39.3 ft)
- 9,000 kg (20,000 lb)

Stegosaurus
- Stegosaurian • USA
- 9 m (29.5 ft) • 3,100 kg (7,000 lb)

Therizinosaurus
- Theropod • Mongolia
- 10 m (33 ft)
- 5,000 kg (11,000 lb)

Utahraptor
- Theropod
- USA
- 7 m (23 ft)
- 500 kg (1,100 lb)

Struthiomimus
- Ornithomimosaur • Canada
- 4 m (13 ft)
- 300 kg (660 lb)

Torosaurus
- Ceratopsian • North America
- 8 m (26 ft) • 4,500 kg (10,000 lb)

Velociraptor
- Theropod • Mongolia
- 2 m (6.5 ft) • 15 kg (33 lb)

Styracosaurus
- Ceratopsian
- Canada
- 5.5 m (18 ft)
- 2,250 kg (5,000 lb)

Triceratops
- Ceratopsian
- USA
- 9 m (29.5 ft)
- 11,000 kg (24,000 lb)

Suchomimus
- Theropod • Niger
- 10 m (32.8 ft) • 2,700 kg (6,000 lb)

Troodon
- Theropod • USA
- 2.5 m (8.2 ft) • 50 kg (110 lb)

Zuniceratops
- Ceratopsian • USA
- 3 m (9.8 ft) • 125 kg (275 lb)

Glossary

Here are the meanings of some words about dinosaurs that are useful to know!

amphibians Cold-blooded vertebrates that have moist skin, lay their eggs in water, and can live in both water and on land, such as newts or frogs

binocular vision Eyesight where both eyes move together to look at the same object to produce a single, clear image

canine teeth Pointed teeth found near the front of the mouth in mammals, used to help capture and eat prey

carnivores Animals that survive by mostly eating the flesh of other animals

ceratopsians Mostly four-legged, plant-eating, and horned dinosaurs with large frills and spikes on their heads

chevrons Series of small, V-shaped bones on the bottom of the tail of most reptiles, many dinosaurs, and some mammals

cold-blooded These animals can only control their body temperature by using an outside source to heat up or cool down

Cretaceous One of the three time periods of the Mesozoic Era, lasting from about 145–66 million years ago

dromaeosaurs Meaning "running lizards", this group of dinosaurs are better known as raptors. They had feathers and sharp claws and teeth used for hunting

extinction When all members of a species of living thing have died out, they are thought of as extinct

fossils Inorganic remains of a plant or animal that lived at least 10,000 years ago. Fossils include skeletons, impressions, and footprints

gastroliths Small stones and rocks that are swallowed in order to help digestion by grinding plant material inside the stomach

hadrosaurs Varied group of duck-billed and head-crested dinosaurs that lived 86–66 million years ago

herbivores Animals that survive by finding and feeding on plant material, including leaves, roots and seeds

Hesperosuchus Early ancestor of the crocodile that lived about 220 million years ago

integument Non-bony structures that cover an animal's skeleton, which can include skin, scales, feathers, and shells

invertebrates Animals that do not have a spinal column, such as insects, worms, jellyfish, and spiders

Jurassic Second of the three time periods of the Mesozoic Era, lasting from about 201–145 million years ago

keratin Strong material that is the main substance in fingernails, horns, hooves, nails, claws, and bills

mammals Vertebrate animals with fur or hair, which are fed by milk from the mother when young, such as dogs and bears

maniraptorans Group of small, primarily meat-eating dinosaurs that had feathers and evolved into modern birds

Mesozoic This era, when the dinosaurs lived, ran from about 252–66 million years ago. The Mesozoic is divided into the Triassic, Jurassic, and Cretaceous periods

nasal bones Bones related to the nasal column that form the bridge of the nose

neural spines Large, flat extensions of the spine that point up and away from an animal's back

omnivores Animals that have evolved to eat all types of food, including other animals, plants, insects and fish

opposable fifth finger Finger that can turn back against the other fingers, giving an animal the ability to grasp things with the hand

ornithomimids Ostrich-like dinosaurs that walked on two legs. Many of them had feathers, and were amongst the fastest running dinosaurs

ornithopods Very successful group of two-legged dinosaurs that used specialized teeth to eat food

osteoderms Bony plates and knobs under the skin that act as armour and help in protection from predators

paleontology Science and study of life forms that existed before the appearance of humans. Paleontologists use fossils in their work

Permian Time period just before the appearance of dinosaurs. It spans about 299–252 million years ago

predator Any animal that gets food by eating other animals. Predators include lions, wolves, and killer whales

prey An animal that is hunted and killed by another animal for food

prosauropods Smaller and often able to walk on two legs, these plant-eating dinosaurs developed into sauropods

protofeathers Downy tufts that provided warmth and evolved into full-sized feathers used for flight

pterosaurs Warm-blooded flying reptiles that lived alongside dinosaurs in the Mesozoic Era

reptiles Vertebrates that live on land, which are cold-blooded and have scaly skin, such as snakes and lizards

riparian Area on and around the banks of a river or stream, which can support a large number of different species

sauropods Dinosaurs with five toes, long necks, and long tails. Sauropods are the largest land animals of all time

scavenge To gather or search an area for something, particularly food

serrated Notched and saw-like edges, like a knife. Usually used for cutting and shearing

sickle-shaped Curved and hook-like, usually for use in slashing and cutting

stereoscopic vision Three-dimensional vision that allows an animal to see layers of depth and distance

tendons Strong bands of tissue that are found throughout the body and attach muscles to bones

theropods Three-toed, mainly meat-eating dinosaurs that walked on two legs. They are now represented by all living birds

thumb spike Sharp point made of bone that is found in place of a thumb in some animals, often as a weapon

Triassic One of the three time periods of the Mesozoic Era, lasting from about 252–201 million years ago

vegetation All of the plants and plant life found in a particular area

vertebrates Animals that have a backbone or spine and a brain enclosed within a skull, such as mammals and birds

warm-blooded These animals are able to control body temperature internally, through actions such as sweating or shivering

Index

Acknowledgements

The publisher would like to thank the following for their assistance in the preparation of this book: Jaileen Kaur and Romi Chakraborty (design), Vijay Kandwal (DTP design), and Sakshi Saluja (Picture research).

The publisher would like to thank the following for their kind permission to reproduce their photographs:

(Key: a-above; b-below/bottom; c-centre; f-far; l-left; r-right; t-top)

2 Alamy Stock Photo: Elena Elenaphotos21 (bc). **7 Dorling Kindersley:** Natural History Museum, London (cla). **9 Getty Images:** Nobumichi Tamara / Stocktrek Images (c). **12-13 Alamy Stock Photo:** Eye Risk. **16 Dreamstime.com:** Leonello Calvetti (b). **18-19 Alamy Stock Photo:** Chrisstockphotography. **24-25 Alamy Stock Photo:** Friedrich Saurer (b). **27 Getty Images:** Nobumichi Tamara / Stocktrek Images (b). **30 Dreamstime.com:** Corey A. Ford. **45 Dreamstime.com:** Corey A. Ford. **46-47 Alamy Stock Photo:** Elena Elenaphotos21. **46 Dreamstime.com:** Corey A. Ford (cla). **50 Dorling Kindersley:** Jon Hughes (cr). **Getty Images:** Nobumichi Tamara / Stocktrek Images (cra). **50-51 Dorling Kindersley:** Ed Merritt / Dorling Kindersley. **51 Getty Images:** Nobumichi Tamara / Stocktrek Images (ca). **64-65 Getty Images:** SCIEPRO. **65 Alamy Stock Photo:** Stocktrek Images, Inc. (b). **66 Dorling Kindersley:** Roby Braun / Gary Ombler (tl). **67 Dorling Kindersley:** Jon Hughes (cr). **68-69 Getty Images:** Nobumichi Tamara / Stocktrek Images. **72 Alamy Stock Photo:** Reynold Sumayku (clb). **72-73 Dorling Kindersley:** Royal Tyrrell Museum of Palaeontology, Alberta, Canada. **73 Dorling Kindersley:** Natural History Museum, London (tr). **82-83 Alamy Stock Photo:** Stocktrek Images, Inc.. **83 Dreamstime.com:** Corey A. Ford (b). **84-85 Dorling Kindersley:** Jon Hughes. **84 Dorling Kindersley:** David Peart (bl); Linda Pitkin (bc). **92 Alamy Stock Photo:** Stocktrek Images, Inc. (bl). **96-97 Getty Images:** Photographer's Choice RF / Jon Boyes. **97 Getty Images:** Nobumichi Tamura / Stocktrek Images (br). **98 Dorling Kindersley:** Jon Hughes (cla). **110 Dorling Kindersley:** Natural History Museum (bl). **131 Photolibrary:** Photodisc / White (cla). **133 Alamy Stock Photo:** Ray Wilson (b). **134 Alamy Stock Photo:** Eye Risk (cla); Friedrich Saurer (cra). **Dreamstime.com:** Corey A. Ford (br); Leonello Calvetti (ca). **Getty Images:** Nobumichi Tamara / Stocktrek Images (crb). **135 Alamy Stock Photo:** Elena Elenaphotos21 (cr/Deinocheirus). **Dreamstime.com:** Corey A. Ford (cra). **136 Alamy Stock Photo:** Stocktrek Images, Inc. (cr). **Dorling Kindersley:** Roby Braun / Gary Ombler (cl). **Getty Images:** SCIEPRO (cra); Nobumichi Tamara / Stocktrek Images (crb). **137 Alamy Stock Photo:** Stocktrek Images, Inc. (cb). **Dreamstime.com:** Corey A. Ford (tr). **138 Alamy Stock Photo:** Stocktrek Images, Inc. (cl). Dorling Kindersley: Jon Hughes (c). **139 Getty Images:** Nobumichi Tamura / Stocktrek Images (tr)

Cover images:
Front: **Dorling Kindersley:** Jon Hughes tc

Poster images:
Dorling Kindersley: Roby Braun / Gary Ombler ca; **Dreamstime.com:** Corey A. Ford clb; **Getty Images:** SCIEPRO cra, Nobumichi Tamara / Stocktrek Images cla

All other images © Dorling Kindersley
For further information see: www.dkimages.com